ADVANCED**CELTIC** FINGERSTYLE GUITAR

Twelve Popular Scottish & Irish Folk Songs Arranged For Solo Acoustic Guitar

DARYL**KELLIE**

FUNDAMENTAL**CHANGES**

Advanced Celtic Fingerstyle Guitar

Twelve Popular Scottish & Irish Folk Songs Arranged For Solo Acoustic Guitar

ISBN: 978-1-78933-211-7

Published by **www.fundamental-changes.com**

Copyright © 2020 Daryl Kellie

Edited by Tim Pettingale

www.fundamental-changes.com

Twitter: **@guitar_joseph**

Over 11,000 fans on Facebook: **FundamentalChangesInGuitar**

Instagram: **FundamentalChanges**

For over 350 Free Guitar Lessons with Videos Check Out

www.fundamental-changes.com

Cover Image Copyright: Ryan Callard, used by permission

Contents

Introduction

I've always loved Celtic music and in this book I bring together a collection of original fingerstyle arrangements for a dozen of the great Irish and Scottish classics.

I learnt many of these songs from my Grandfather, Ronald Kellie, who was well known for bursting into song at the drop of a hat! A great number of these musical endeavours were based on traditional Irish songs – everything from raucous drinking songs (a considerable number of which would perhaps not be suitable for this book!) to beautiful ballads.

Sadly, he is no longer with us, but revisiting these songs has felt like a real tribute to him. I have, of course, arranged and interpreted these songs using modern fingerstyle techniques, but I hope that I have maintained the intention and feel of the original pieces. Arranging and playing them for you to learn has been a real pleasure and I like to think that my Granddad would find the thought of serious guitarists playing a tune like *Reilly's Daughter* very amusing indeed!

This music will always have a special place in my heart. I hope you enjoy it!

Daryl Kellie

May 2020

Get the Audio

The audio files for this book are available to download for free from **www.fundamental-changes.com.** The link is in the top right-hand corner. Simply select this book title from the drop-down menu and follow the instructions to get the audio.

We recommend that you download the files directly to your computer, not to your tablet, and extract them there before adding them to your media library. You can then put them on your tablet, iPod or burn them to CD. On the download page there is a help PDF and we also provide technical support via the contact form.

For over 350 free guitar lessons with videos check out:

www.fundamental-changes.com

Twitter: **@guitar_joseph**

Over 11,000 fans on Facebook: **FundamentalChangesInGuitar**

Instagram: **FundamentalChanges**

See the Videos

You can also check out Daryl Kellie playing selected pieces from the book on the Fundamental Changes website:

https://www.fundamental-changes.com/celtic-classics-performance-videos/

Short link:

https://bit.ly/36n6xNd

Scan with your smartphone:

Chapter One – Planxty Irwin

Planxty Irwin was composed by Turlough O'Carolan (1670-1738). There is some dispute over the origin and meaning of the word "planxty", but it is generally thought to denote a tribute to a particular person. In this case in honour of Colonel John Irwin of Sligo.

This arrangement is in DADGAD tuning with a capo at the 3rd fret. For the introduction, use the picking hand *p i m a* fingers (thumb, index, middle, ring finger) to rapidly alternate between the strings.

Example 1a

In bar thirty-six, notice the use of *Rasgueado* technique (marked "rasg"). This is typically a Spanish guitar technique, but I employ it on some of these arrangements to mimic the fast triplets often played by the bodhrán player. To execute it, first strum in the usual way and hammer-on to fret four. Next, unfurl the fingers from behind the thumb, causing several strums in quick succession. Pull-off to the open first string and finish the bar with a normal strum. Listen to how it sounds on the audio example and focus on this bar in isolation until you've perfected the technique.

Example 1b

Here is the full arrangement.

Planxty Irwin arrangement

Open Dsus4
① = D
② = A
⑥ = D

♩. = 100

Capo fret 3

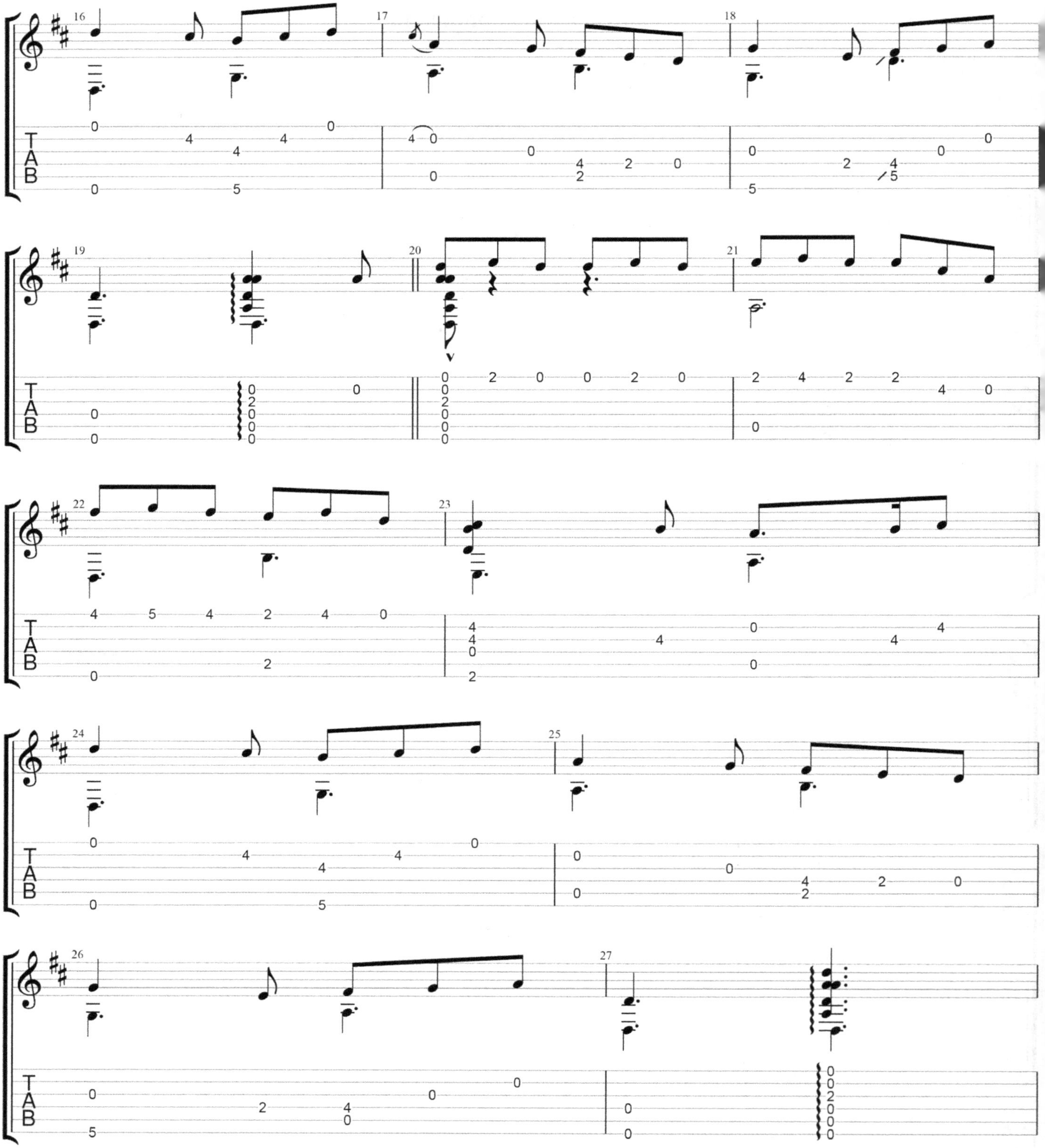

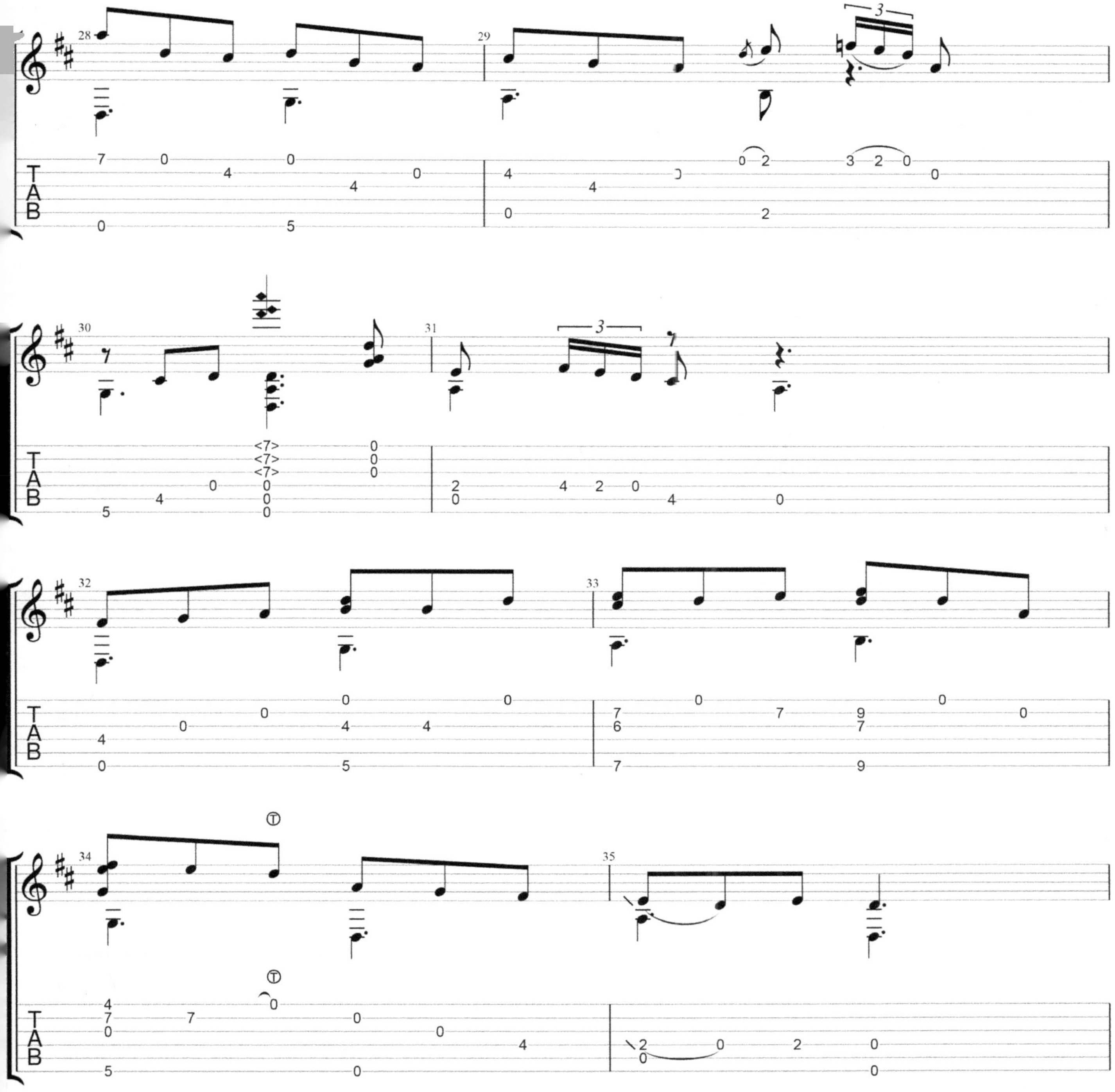

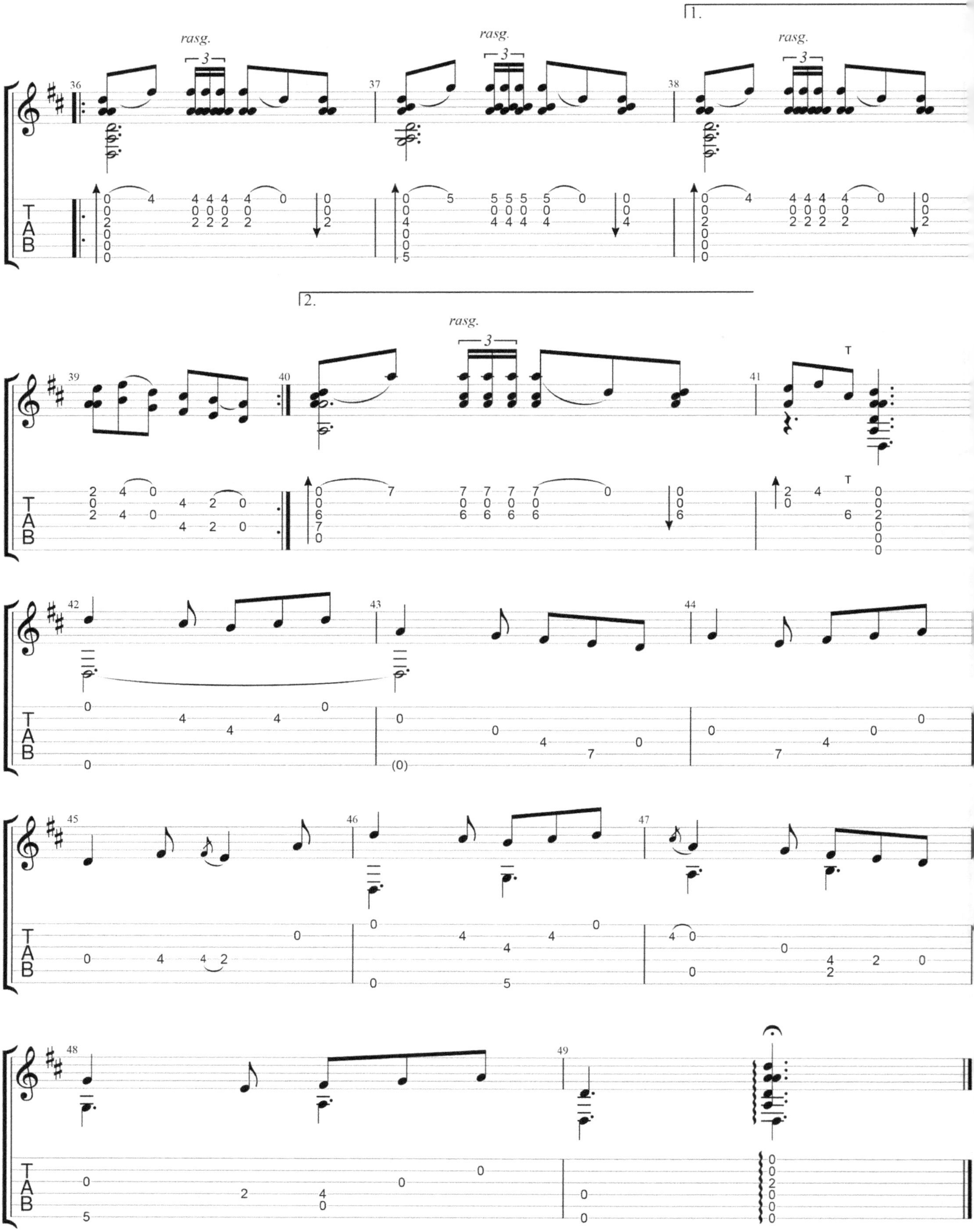
1.
rasg.
rasg.
rasg.
2.
rasg.
T

Chapter Two – Skye Boat Song

This 19th Century Scottish song recalls the journey of Bonnie Prince Charlie to the Isle of Skye to evade capture after the Jacobite uprising of 1745.

This is a fairly straightforward arrangement in DADGAD tuning. In bar twenty-four, pick the fifth and first strings with *p* (thumb) and *a* (ring finger), then use *p* again for the fourth string. After picking the third string with *i* (index) you will need to reposition it over the harmonic node point at the 12th fret and simultaneously pick with *p*. After this, return the picking hand to its original position.

Example 2a

Bar twenty-six features the exact same movements with the right hand, except you will play an artificial harmonic (hence the node point will need to be at the 14th fret).

Example 2b

Now here's the full arrangement.

Skye Boat Song arrangement

Open Dsus4
① = D
② = A
⑥ = D

♩ = 98

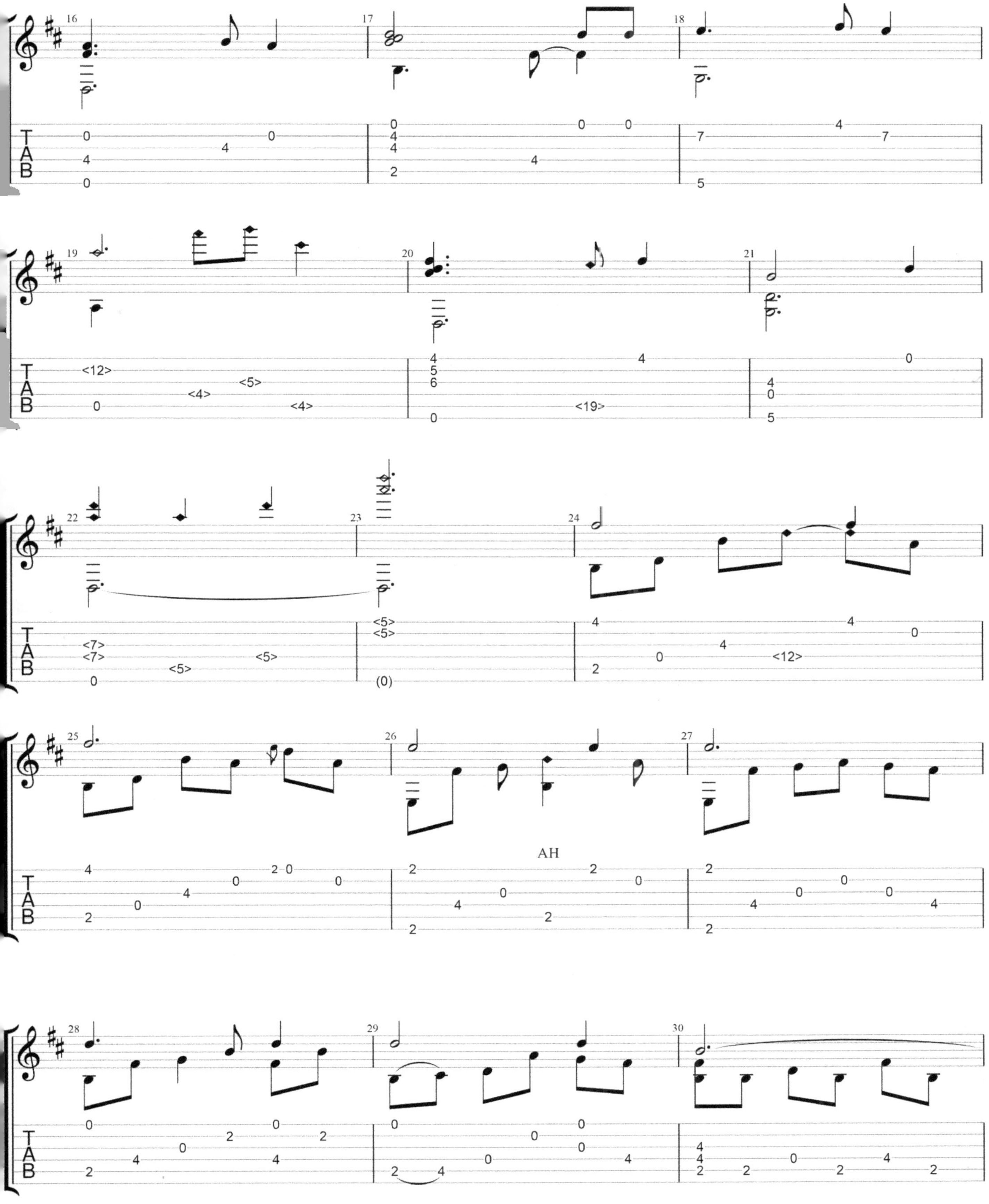
AH

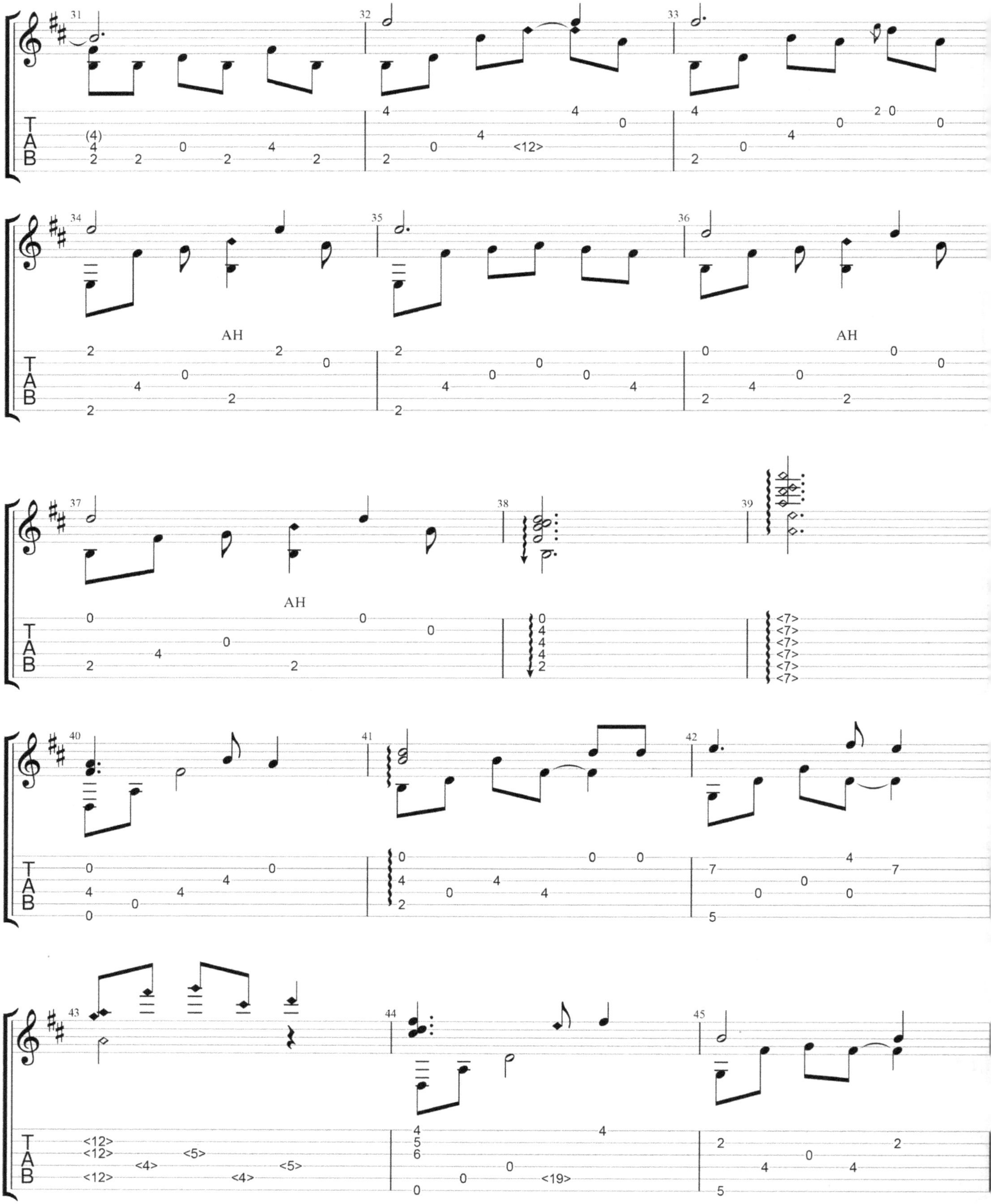
AH
AH
AH

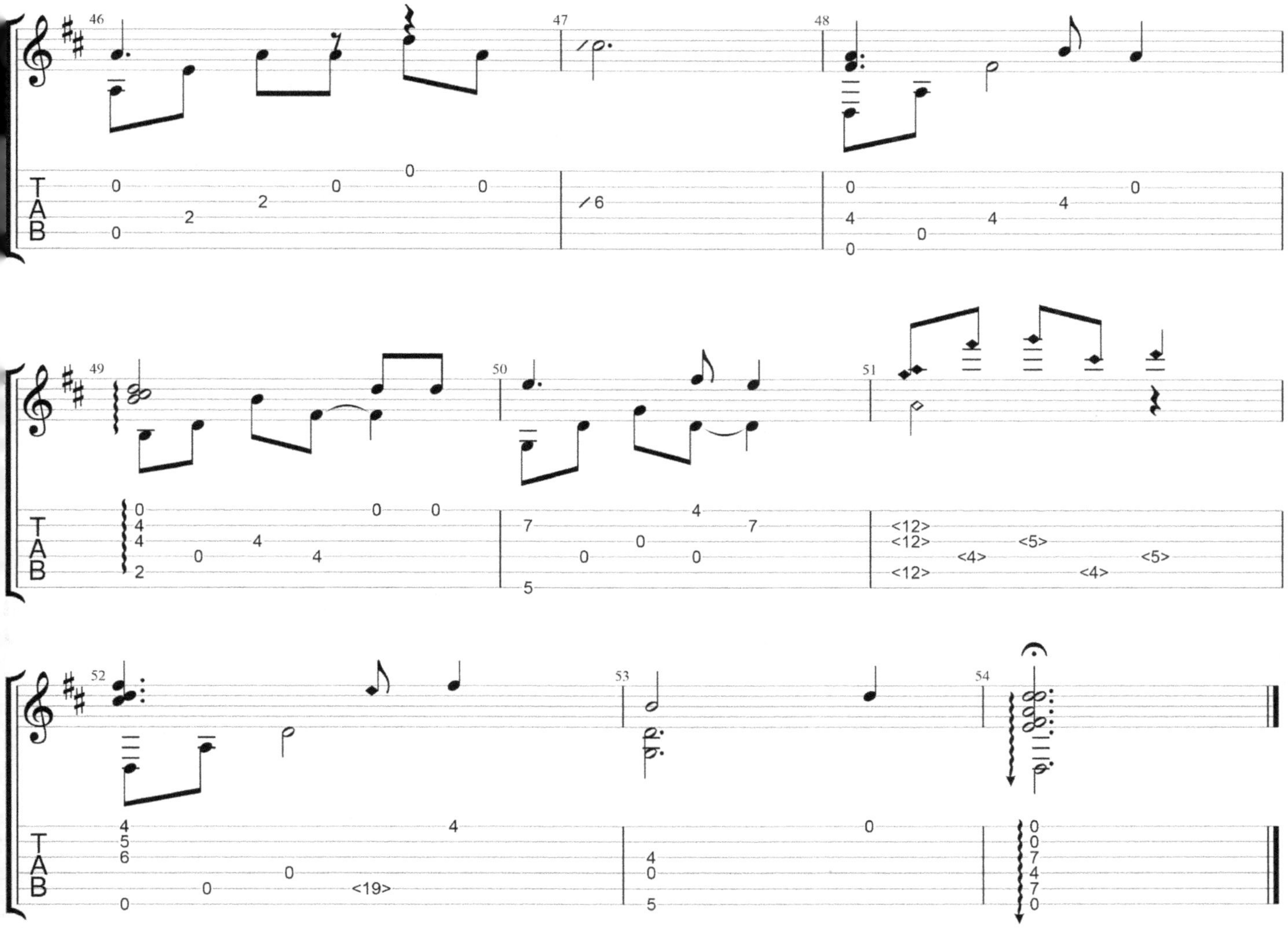

Chapter Three – Cockles and Mussels

Cockles and Mussels (also known as *Molly Malone*) tells the tale of a fishwife trailing her cart through the streets of Dublin. Perhaps one of the most famous folk songs, it is often thought to be the unofficial anthem of Dublin. This arrangement features some unusual techniques with harmonics.

When you encounter these passages, the harmonics are picked with *p* (thumb) as *i* (index) touches the 12th fret, while the notes on the first string are picked with *a* (ring finger). Watch out for the artificial harmonic (marked AH), which will require *i* to touch the node point at the 14th fret.

Example 3a

This idea continues, but will require more fretted notes and therefore more shifting of *i* between the node points on frets 14 and 12. Notice how many of the open strings in this arrangement are sounded by pulling away fingers in the fretting hand (indicated here with a "T").

Example 3b

This fast triplet strum is an example of the "Celtic Rasgueado" technique described in the performance notes for *Planxty Irwin*. Unfurl the fingers from behind the thumb to achieve this series of small, rapid strums. In the following bar use the picking hand *i* finger to fret-tap the notes labelled "T" and *a* to pick the open strings.

Example 3c

The harmonics in Example 3d are all "tapped harmonics". Slap the *m* or *i* finger onto the 12th fret to achieve these. Later, use *i* to fret-tap the notes at the 7th fret (flatten the finger to fret both strings at once), then pull off to sound the open string that follows.

Example 3d

Here is the full arrangement for you.

Cockles and Mussels arrangement

Open Dsus4
① = D
② = A
⑥ = D

𝅘𝅥 = 108

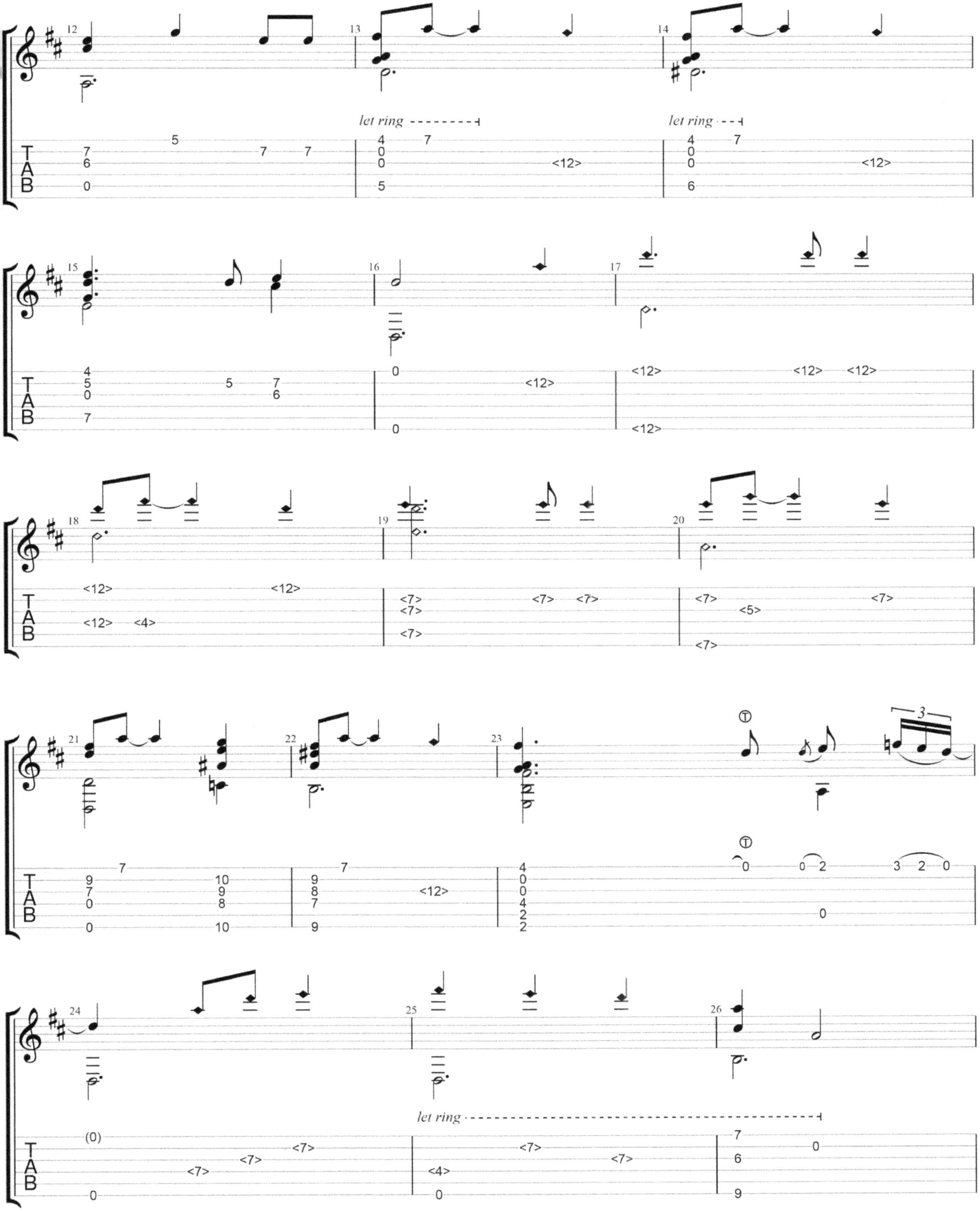
let ring
let ring
let ring

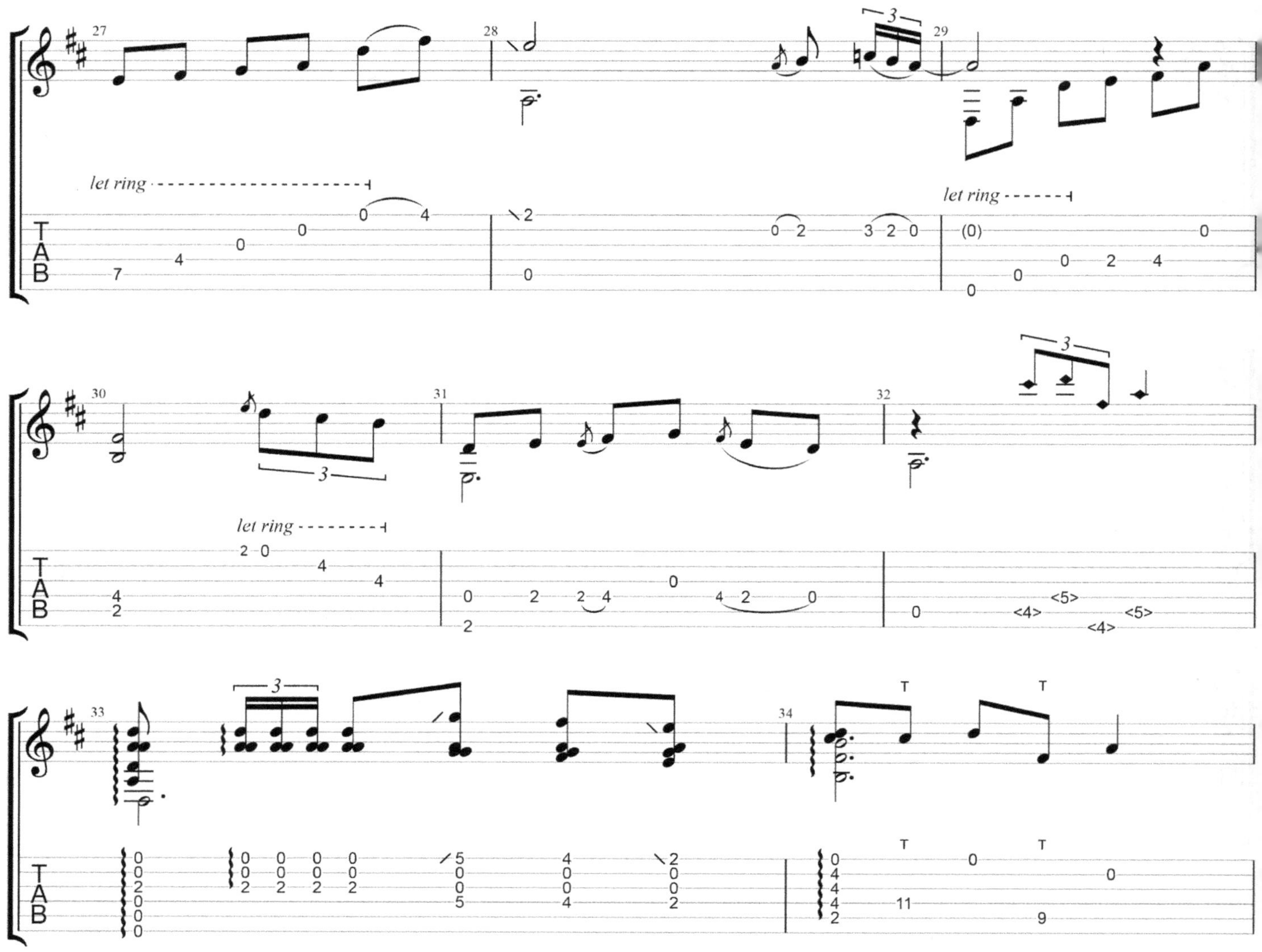
let ring
let ring
let ring
T
T

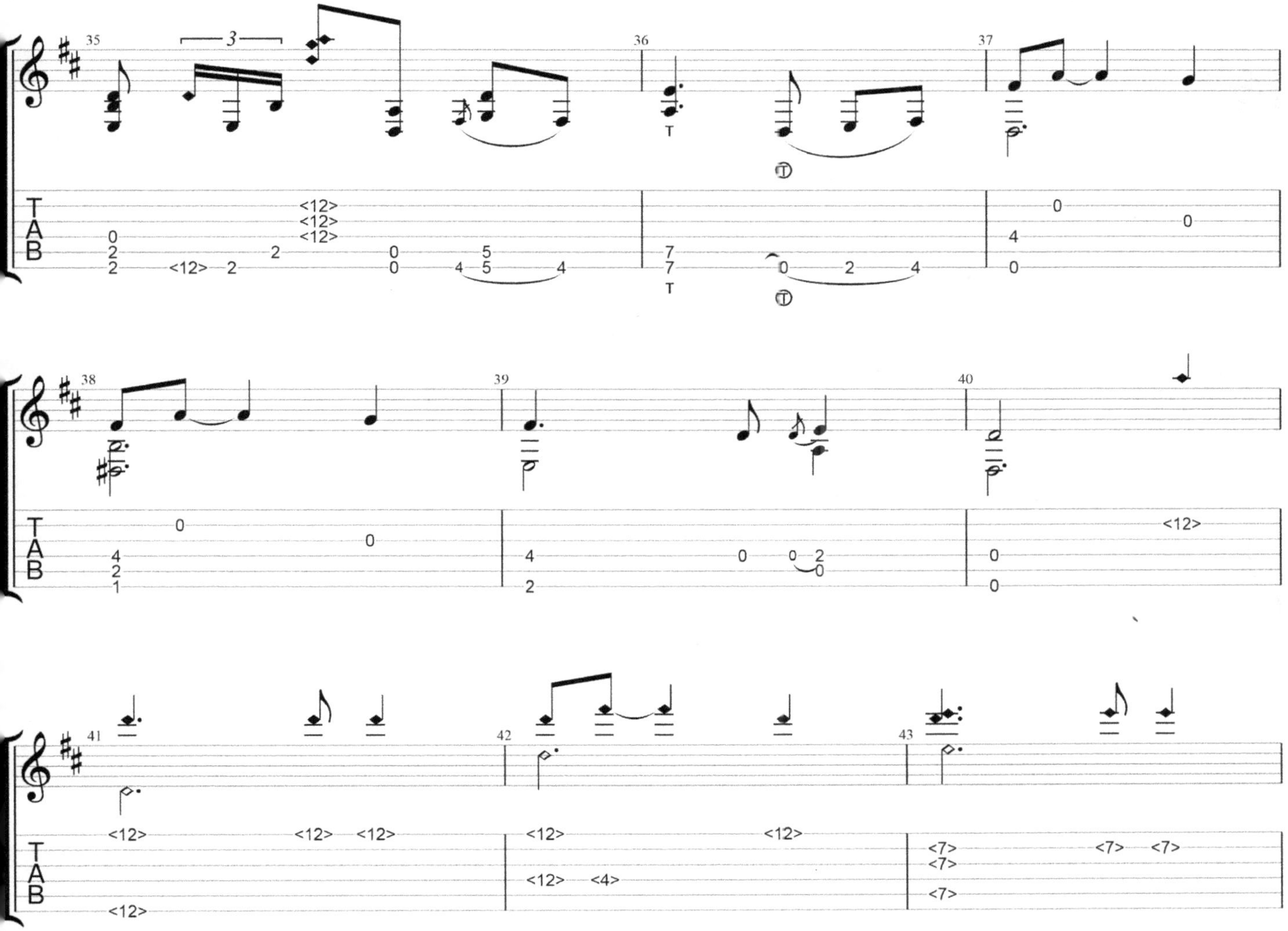
35
36
37
TAB
38
39
40
TAB
41
42
43
TAB

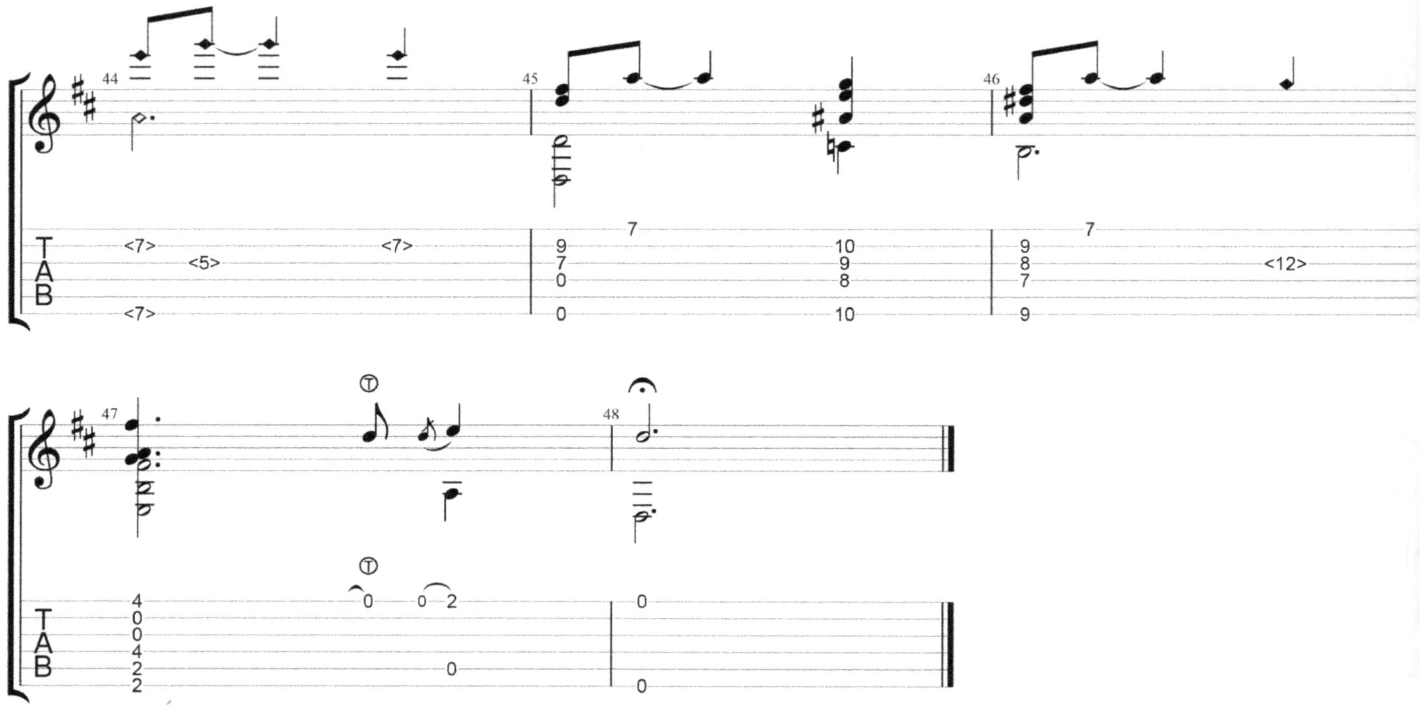

Chapter Four – Drowsy Maggie

Drowsy Maggie is perhaps one of the best-known examples of a "reel". This is a dance tune in common time, rather than in 6/8 (which is known a "jig"). The energetic pace and modal tonality give it a distinctly Celtic sound. For this arrangement, practice slowly at first with a metronome to ensure all of the subtleties and ornaments are reproduced accurately.

The harmonics in bar ten are all natural harmonics, played with the normal two-handed technique. Spread the fretting hand wide and use finger one for notes on the 4th fret, finger two for the 7th fret, and finger four for the 12th fret.

Example 4a

Open Dsus4
① = D
② = A
⑥ = D

♩ = 130

The open first string (marked with "T") is executed by pulling off from the preceding note on the 4th fret.

Example 4b

Open Dsus4
① = D
② = A
⑥ = D

♩ = 130

In bar twenty-three, be sure to stick to the picking hand fingering indicated to ensure swift even movement between the strings.

Example 4c

Do the same for the semiquaver passages in bars twenty-eight and twenty-nine. Take care to ensure that the pull-offs are as clear and even as the picked notes.

Example 4d

Now here's the full arrangement…

Drowsy Maggie arrangement

Open Dsus4
① = D
② = A
⑥ = D

Da Coda

D.C. al Coda

Chapter Five – All For Me Grog

"Grog" was the term used for the daily ration of rum given to sailors in the Royal Navy. Originally a popular drinking song with sailors in the 19th Century, it has since been adopted by folk performers.

In this arrangement, be sure to let the notes on adjacent strings ring into each other. In Example 5a, notice that the fretted notes must sometimes be held on for several bars to achieve this.

Example 5a

The fast triplets like those in bar twenty-nine are played with a picking hand tremolo technique. Use fingers *a*, *m* and *i* in quick succession, followed by *p* (thumb) for the subsequent quaver.

Example 5b

The harmonics in bar thirty-two are tapped harmonics. The 12th fret harmonics in bars thirty-three and thirty-four are played with the picking hand only, but all the harmonics thereafter should be executed with the normal two-handed technique.

Example 5c

Now here's the full arrangement…

All For Me Grog arrangement

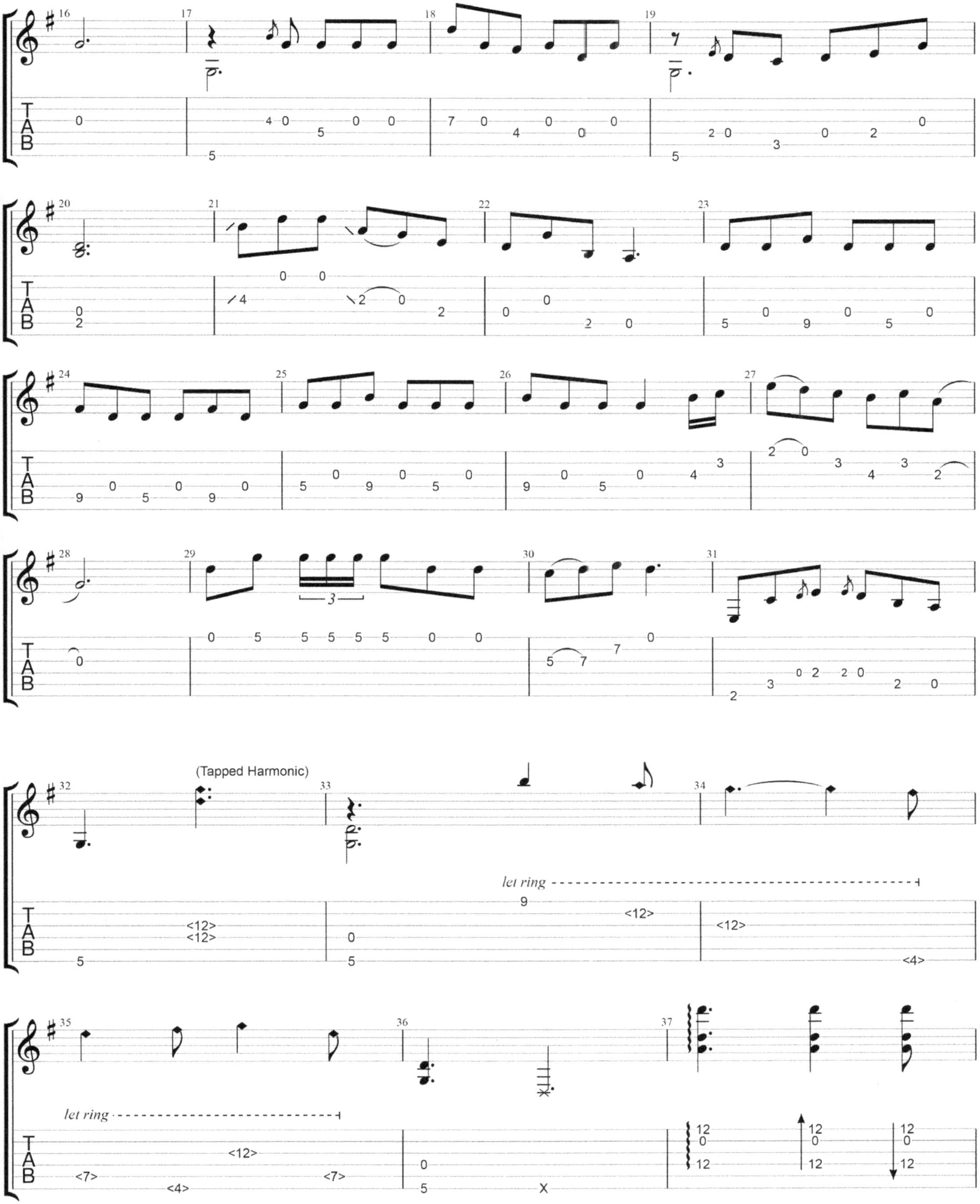
(Tapped Harmonic)
let ring
let ring

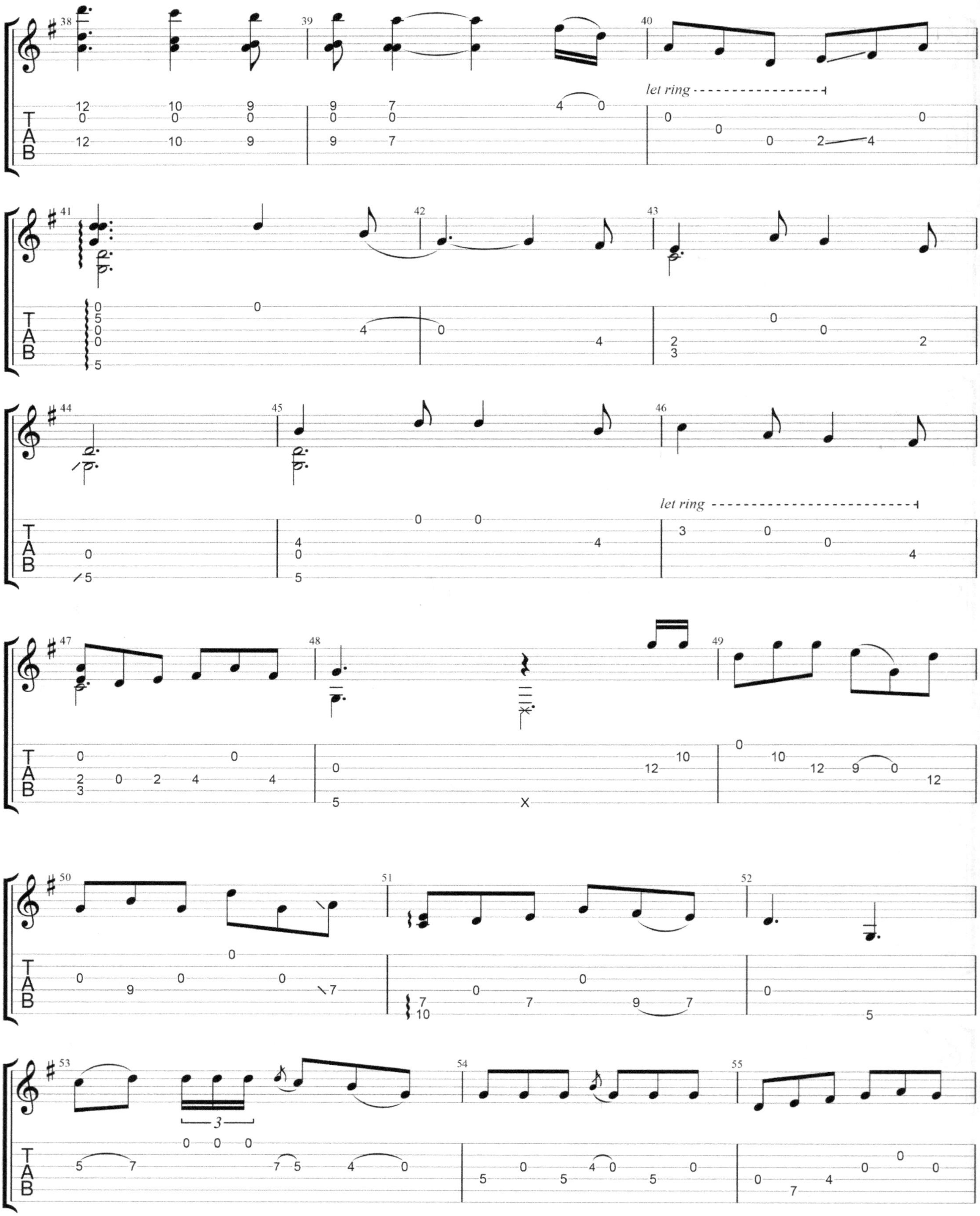
let ring
let ring

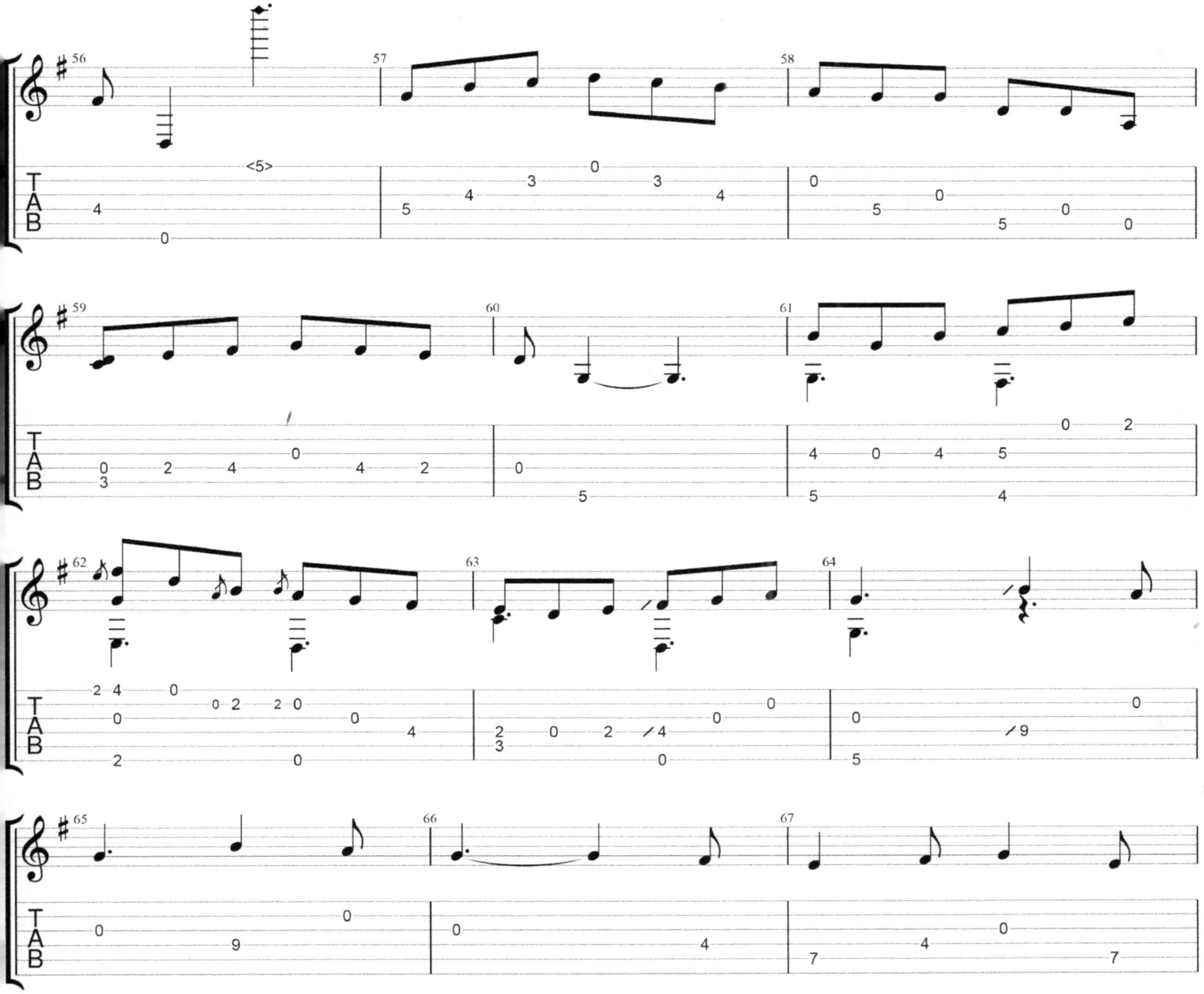

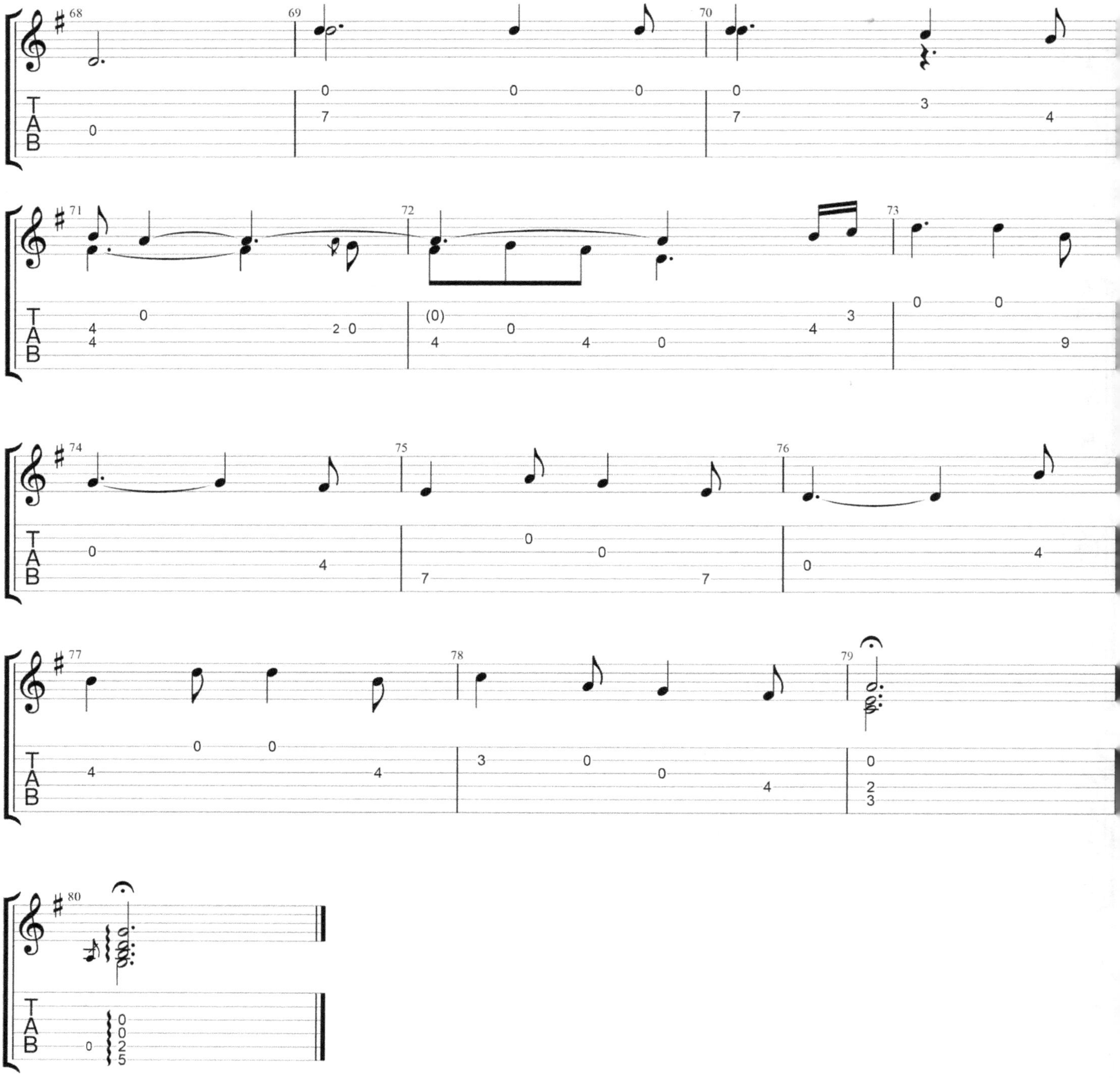
TAB

Chapter Six – Will Ye Go, Lassie, Go?

Will Ye Go, Lassie, Go? (also known as *Wild Mountain Thyme* and *Purple Heather*) is based on the song *The Braes O' Balquhither* by Scottish poet Robert Tannahill (1774–1810) and Scottish composer Robert Archibald Smith (1780–1829). The song was made popular by Irish musician Francis McPeake in the 1950s and has remained a popular ballad on the Folk circuit ever since.

This arrangement is in DADGAD tuning and features a "harp harmonic" introduction.

To play this, begin by holding down the chord shape with the fretting hand on the 4th and 6th fret.

Place the *i* finger over the harmonic node point 12 frets above any fretted notes, or over the 12th fret for any open strings. Pick them with *p* (thumb). Only play the diamond shaped notes this way – pick any other notes normally with *a* (ring finger). Let the notes ring together. The effect should be a lush harp-like sound.

Example 6a

The harmonics in the first bar of Example 6b are tapped harmonics again. Use *m* or *i* to slap the 12th fret to sound them. Those notes marked with a "T" which is not in a circle are normal picking hand fret taps, not harmonics.

Dragging the nail of the ring finger across the strings while keeping the index finger parallel to it over the 19th fret will sound the 19th fret harmonics.

Example 6b

Here's the full arrangement.

Will Ye Go, Lassie, Go? Arrangement

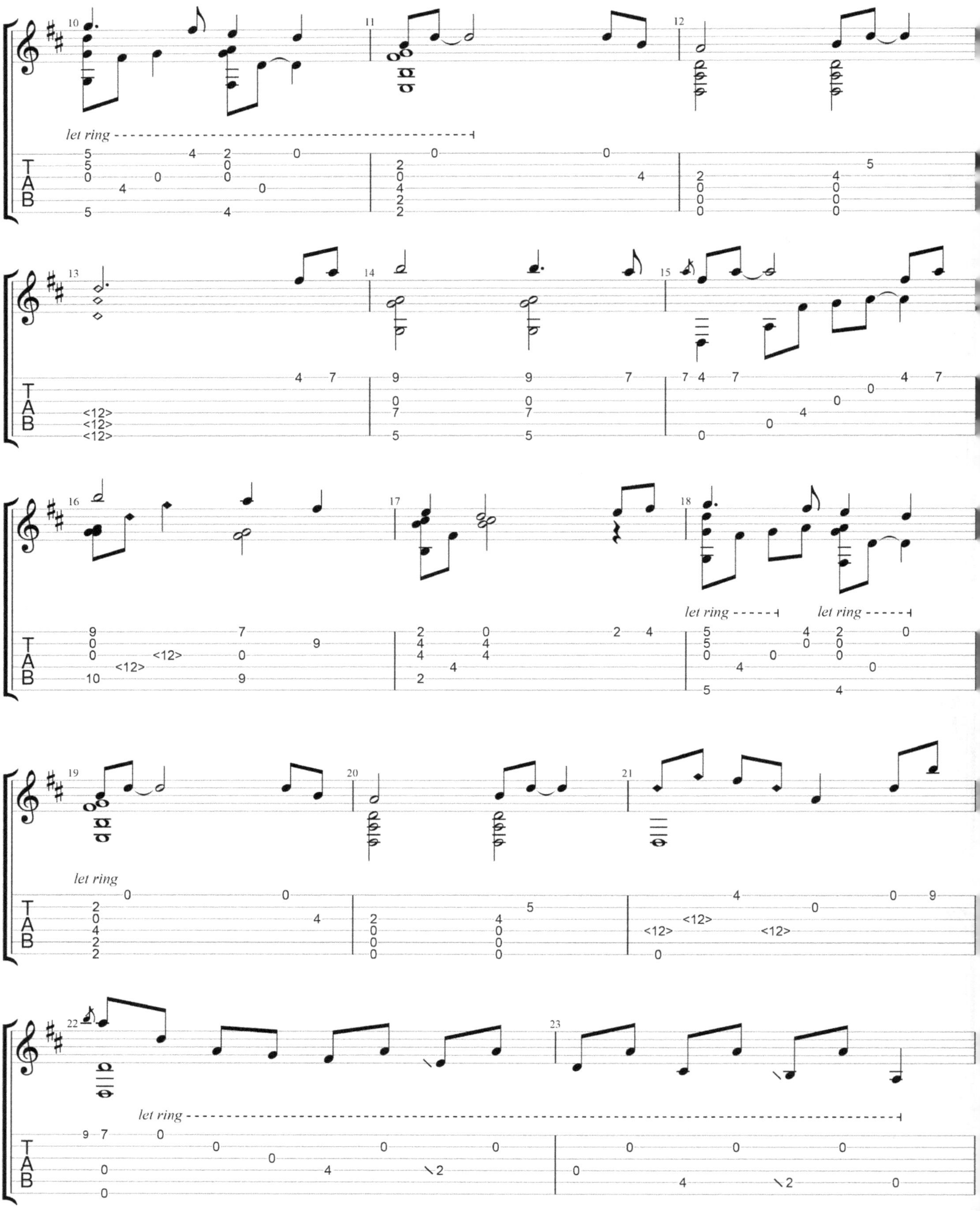
let ring
let ring
let ring
let ring
let ring

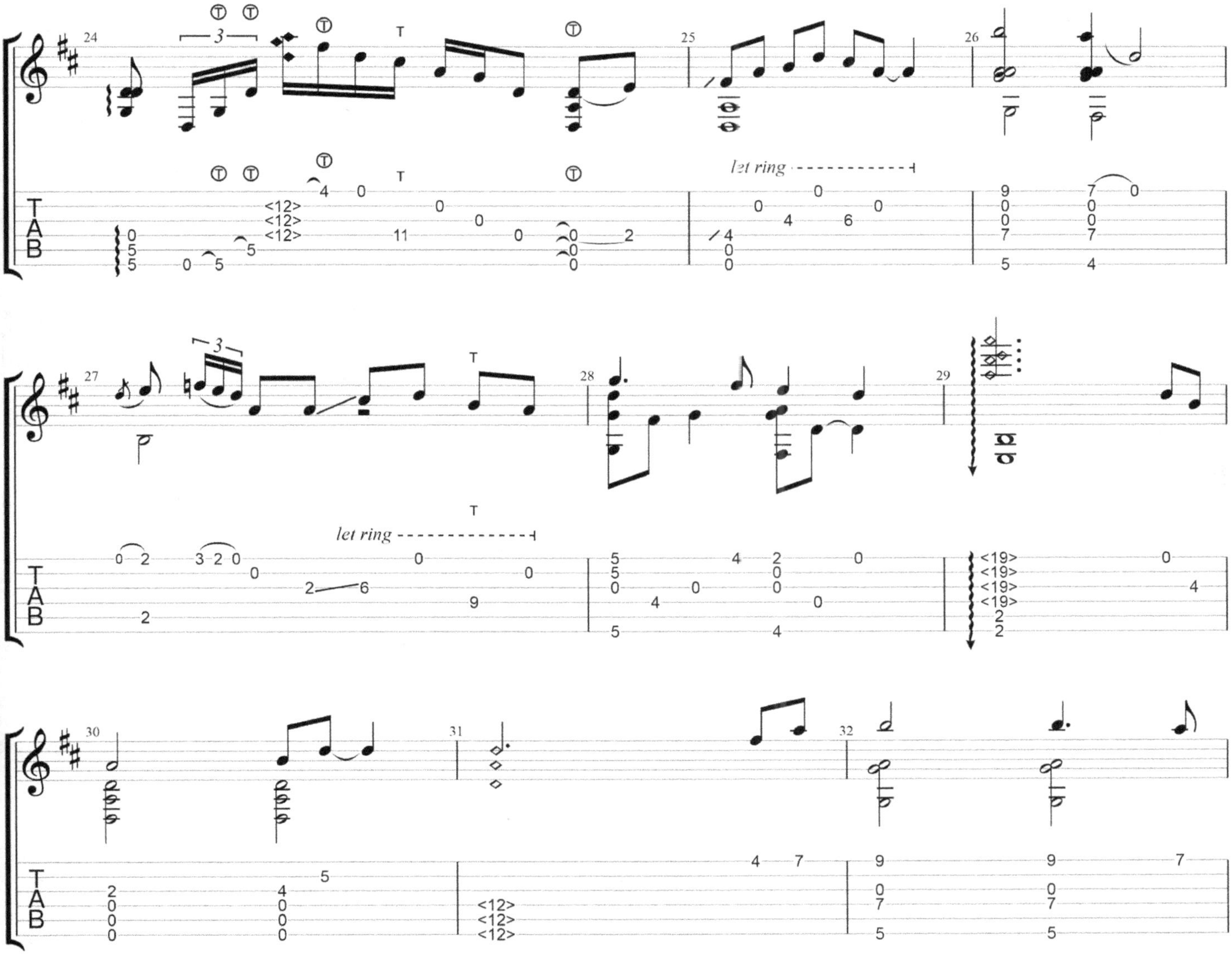
TAB
let ring

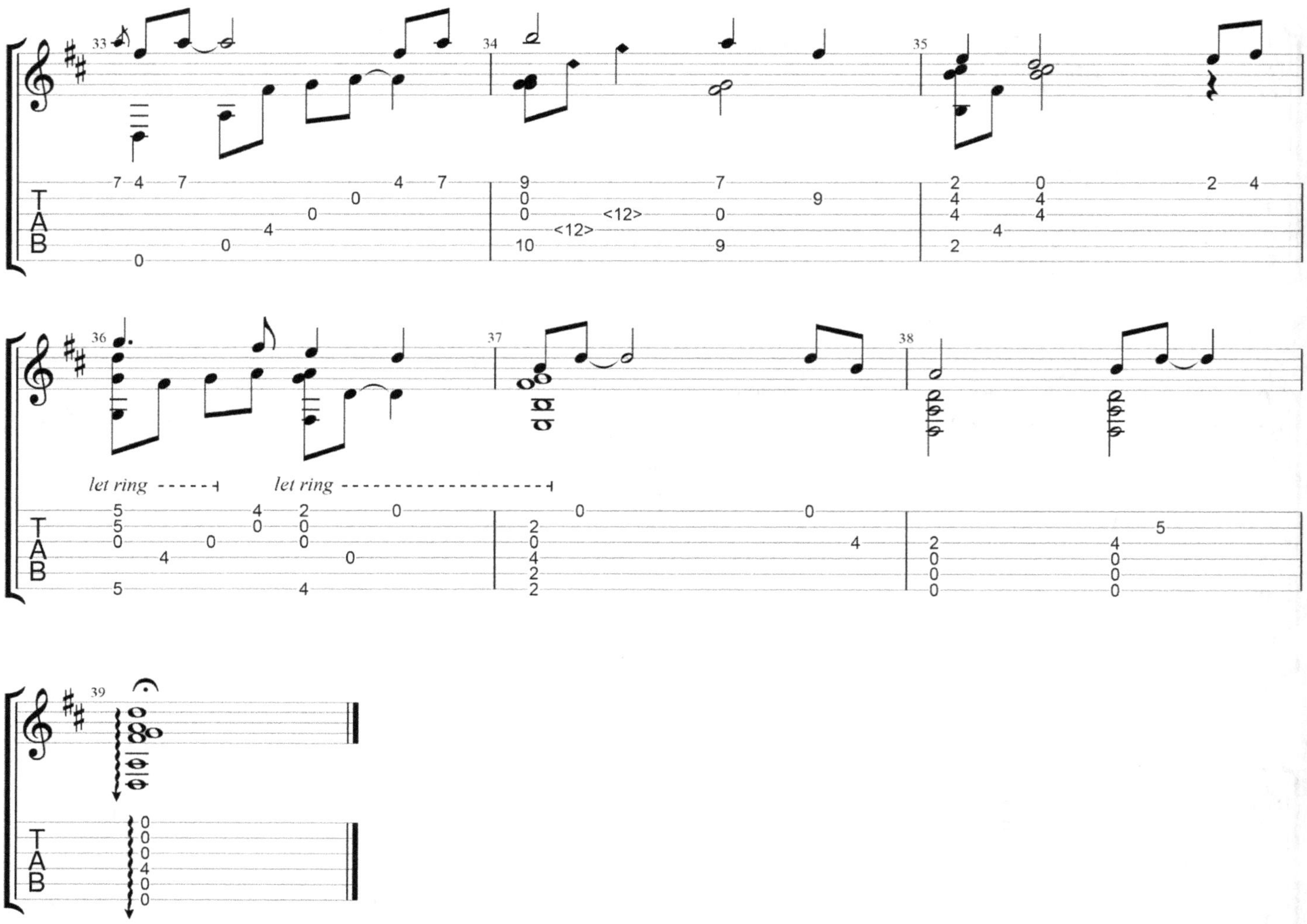
let ring
let ring

Chapter Seven – Reilly's Daughter

This is an old and lively ballad. The verses deal with the story of the pursuit of a beautiful young woman by many a man, each of whom had to contend with her wild and dangerous father!

This arrangement is in open D tuning with a capo at the 3rd fret. The opening lick is played with consecutive notes on adjacent strings to allow them to ring together. The picking pattern from bar two requires the thumb to alternate between the low strings, as the fingers pick out the melody on the high strings. As with all "Travis picking" patterns of this kind, I use a thumb pick and maintain a slight palm mute on the low strings.

Example 7a

From bar eighteen, the alternate picking with the thumb continues, but a harmonic is played at the 19th fret. To play this, position the *i* finger over the node point on the 19th fret and pick with *a*, leaving the thumb free to continue picking. (The note on the third string just before the harmonic is picked with *i*).

Example 7b

Now here's the full arrangement.

Reilly's Daughter arrangement

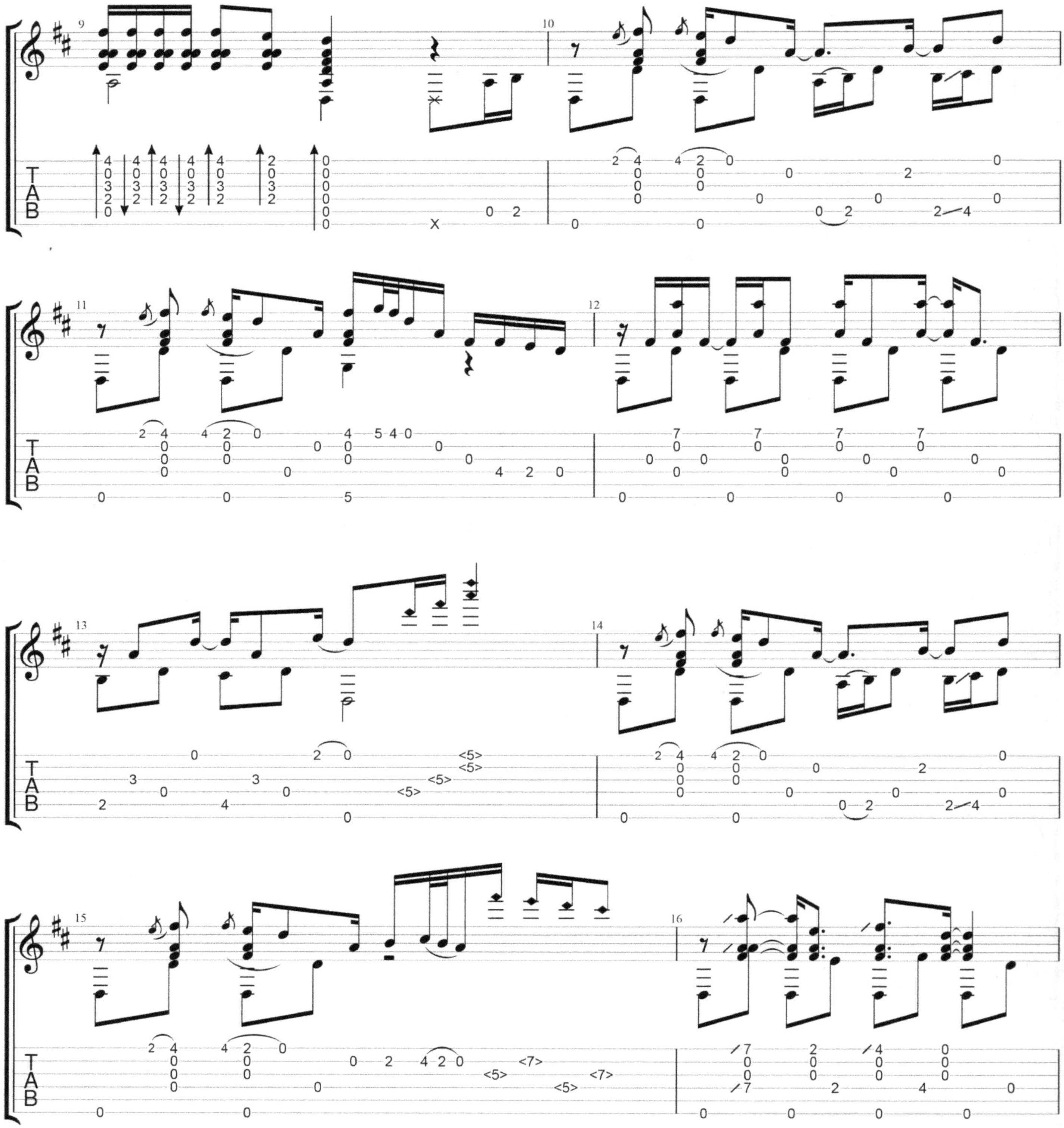

D.S. al Coda

Chapter Eight – Carrickfergus

Carrickfergus is a popular folk song named after the town Carrickfergus in County Antrim, Northern Ireland. The origins of the song are unclear, but the melody has been traced back to the 18th Century Irish language song *Do Bhí Bean Uasal* (*There Was a Noblewoman*). In its modern form it has been performed by everyone from Joan Baez to Bryan Ferry.

The song is often played in 3/4 time, but many popular recordings of the song are in 4/4. Here, it is arranged in 3/4 in DGDGAD tuning.

Much of this arrangement is a straightforward melody on the high strings and simple broken-chord accompaniment underneath. However, in bar thirty-six you will need to do a couple of quick position shifts. Use the fourth finger on the 14th fret, then slide it back to the 12th fret immediately after.

Example 8a

In bar forty-four, be sure to let the natural and artificial harmonics ring together. The node points for the artificial harmonics will be on the 17th and 15th frets (12 frets above frets 5 and 3), so the picking hand movement between these and the node point for the 19th fret natural harmonics will be fairly small.

Example 8b

To finish, let the last few notes ring together (by holding on the fretted notes) into the ending artificial harmonic.

Example 8c

Here is the full arrangement.

Carrickfergus arrangement

Da Coda

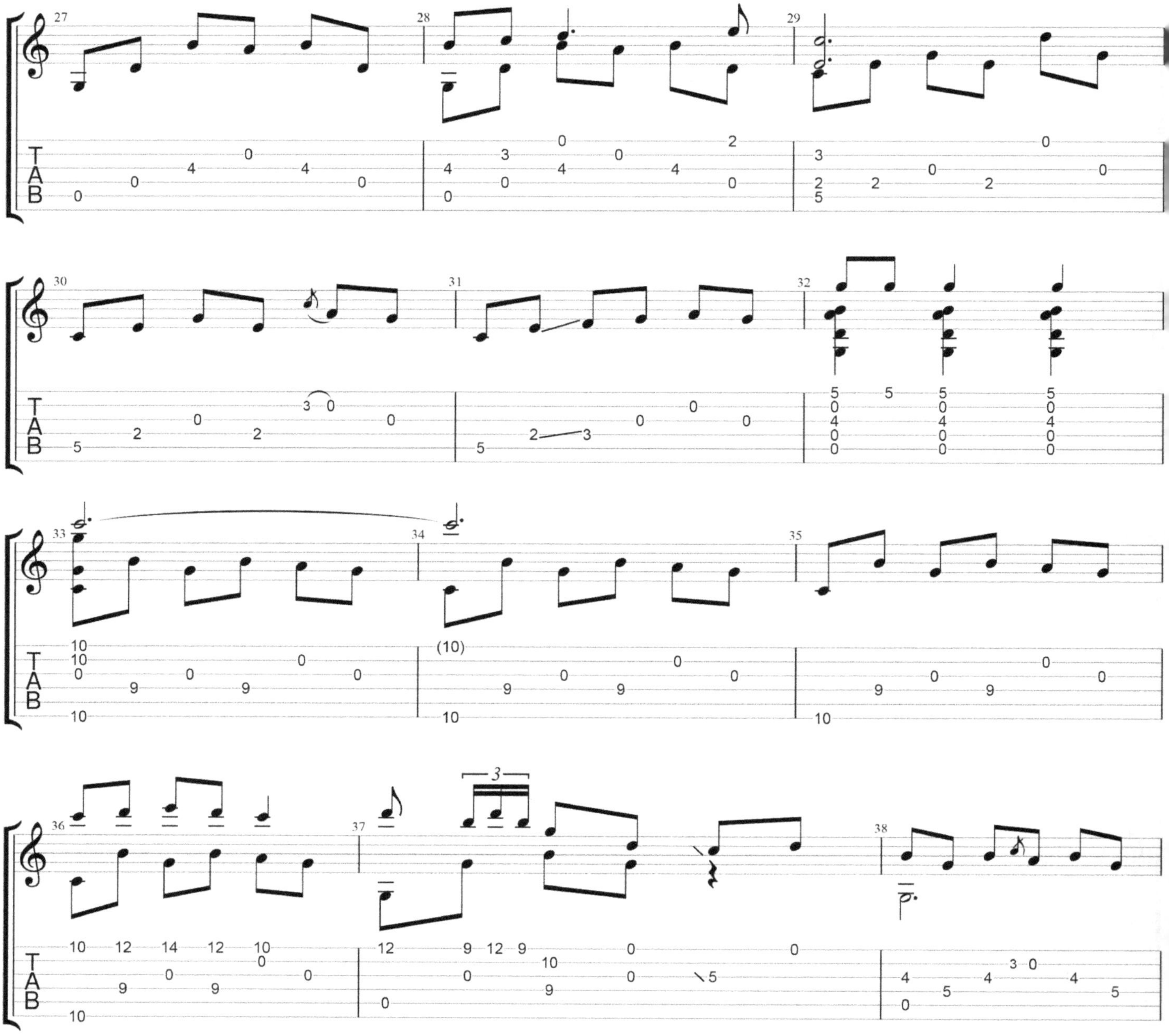

D.C. al Coda

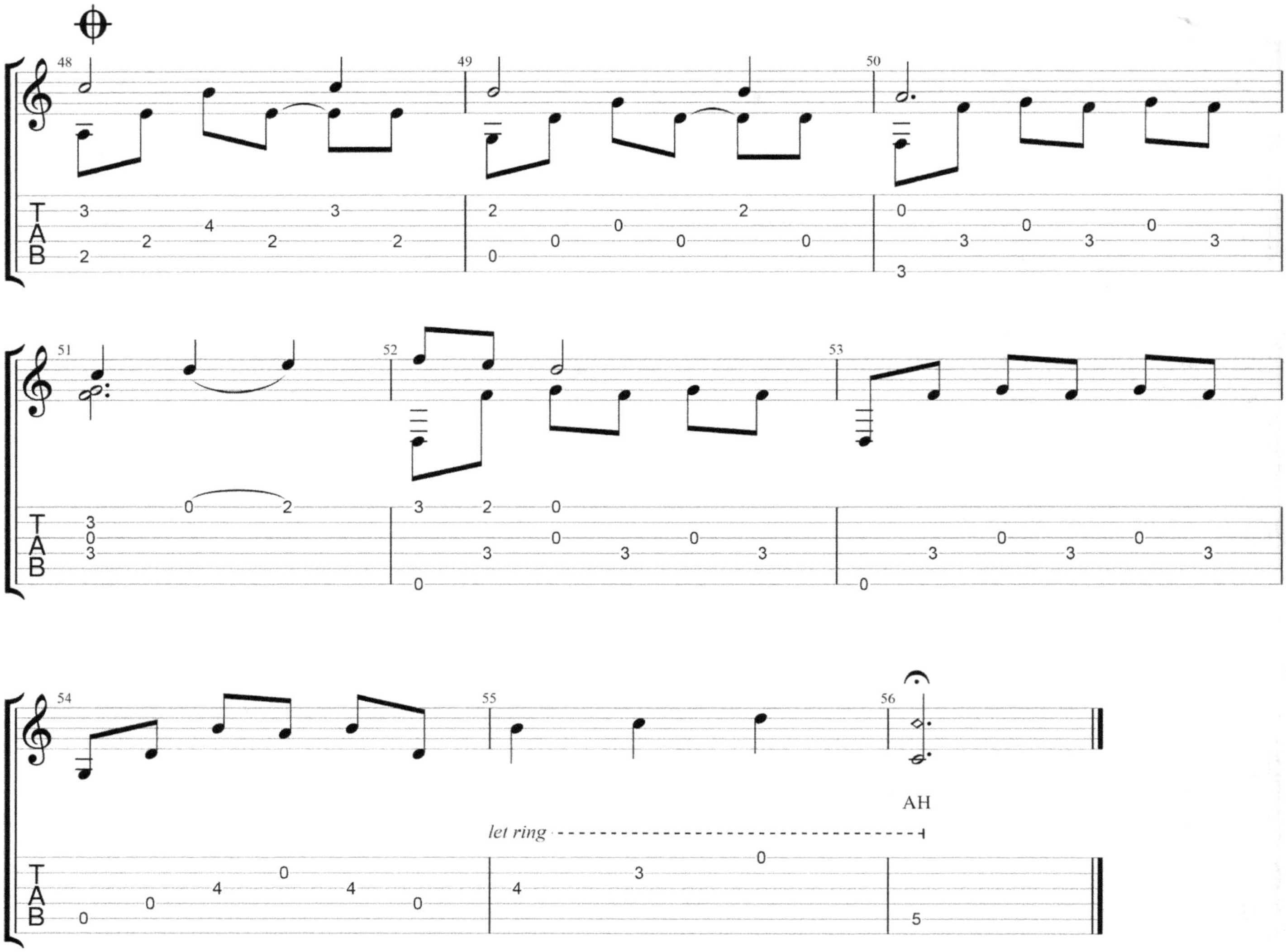
AH
let ring

Chapter Nine – Down by the Sally Gardens

Down by the Sally Gardens (sometimes spelled *Salley*) is based on a poem by W.B. Yeats, first published in 1889. The verse was subsequently set to the melody of the traditional air *The Maids of Mourne Shore*. "Salley" comes from the Gaelic word "saileach" which means "willow". "Sally gardens" therefore simply means willow gardens.

This arrangement is in CGDGAD tuning. In Example 9a, after playing the initial chord, use the harp harmonic technique to alternate between artificial harmonics and the 7th fret non-harmonic notes. The 12th fret harmonics that follow are natural harmonics, played with the normal two-handed technique.

Example 9a

This arrangement has many examples of harmonic and non-harmonic lines played simultaneously. When the harmonic part is on the lower strings (i.e. in bar twenty-one) use *p* thumb to pick and *i* (index) over the node point, with *a* (ring finger) picking the melody on the high strings. When the harmonic is above and a non-harmonic below (i.e. in bar twenty-two, beat 3) use *a* to pick the harmonic with *i* over the node and *p* playing the open low string.

Example 9b

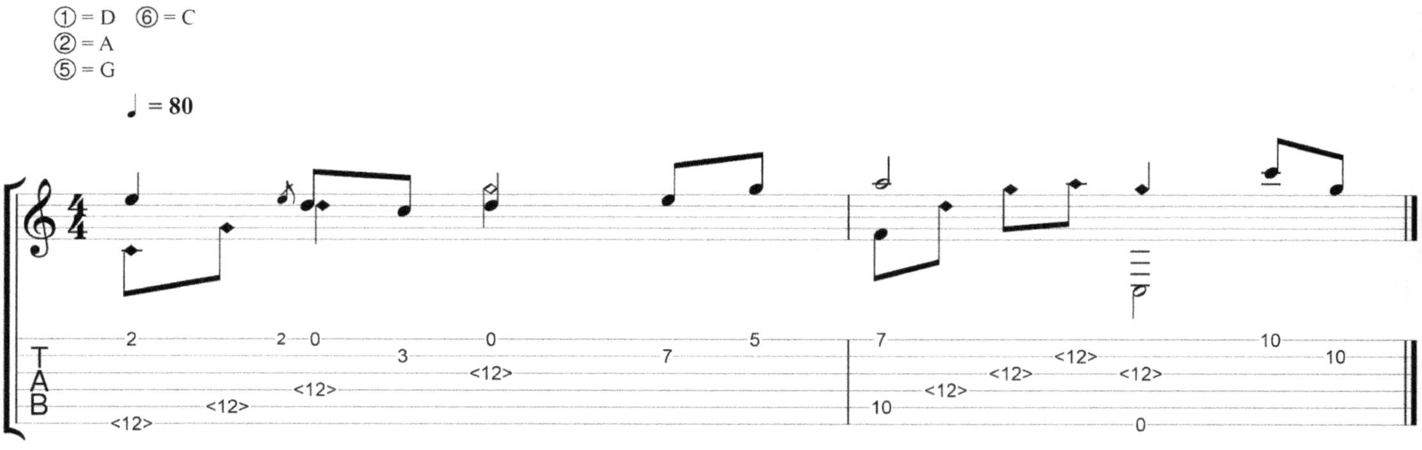

Here's the full arrangement for you.

Down by the Sally Gardens arrangement

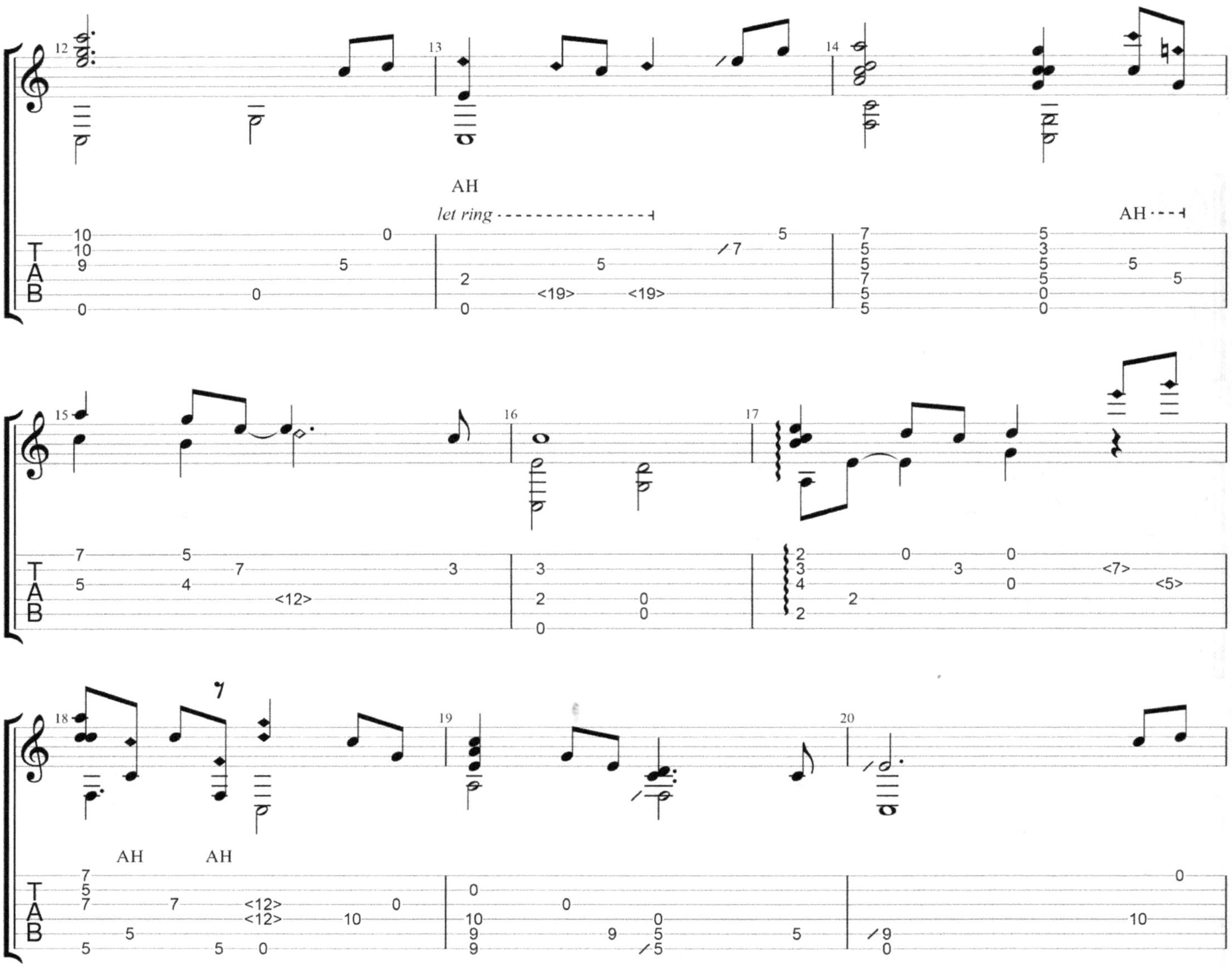
AH
let ring
AH
TAB
AH
AH

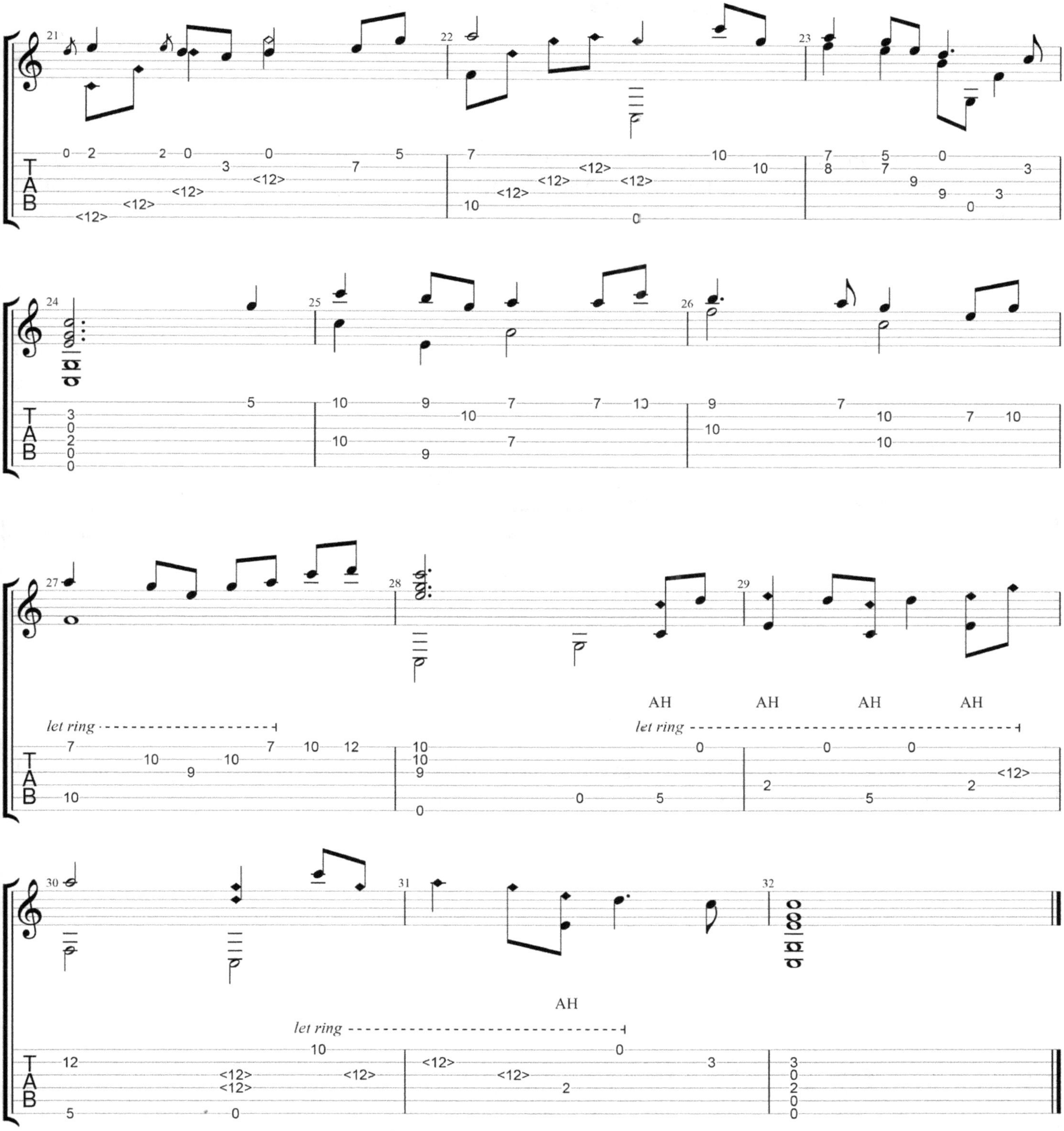
let ring
AH
AH
AH
AH
let ring
AH
let ring

Chapter Ten – Harvest Home

Harvest Home (also known as *The Cork Hornpipe* or *Baile an Fhómhair* by people who prefer its Irish name) refers to the place where people would gather to play music, dance and tell stories at the end of the harvest season.

This arrangement is in dropped D tuning with a capo at the 3rd fret. The section starting at bar twelve features a fast, even succession of notes on the third string. Alternate between *m*, *i* and *p* in the way that a Spanish guitarist would when executing the tremolo technique.

Example 10a

Throughout the arrangement there are passages with notes played on adjacent strings in order to allow them to ring together. This is fairly easy to do, just remember to hold any fretted notes down for as long as possible.

Example 10b

Although using harmonics when employing the tremolo technique may at first seem daunting, the technique is exactly the same as that described in Example 10a. Just alternate between *m*, *i* and *p* on the third string.

Example 10c

Now here's the full arrangement...

Harvest Home arrangement

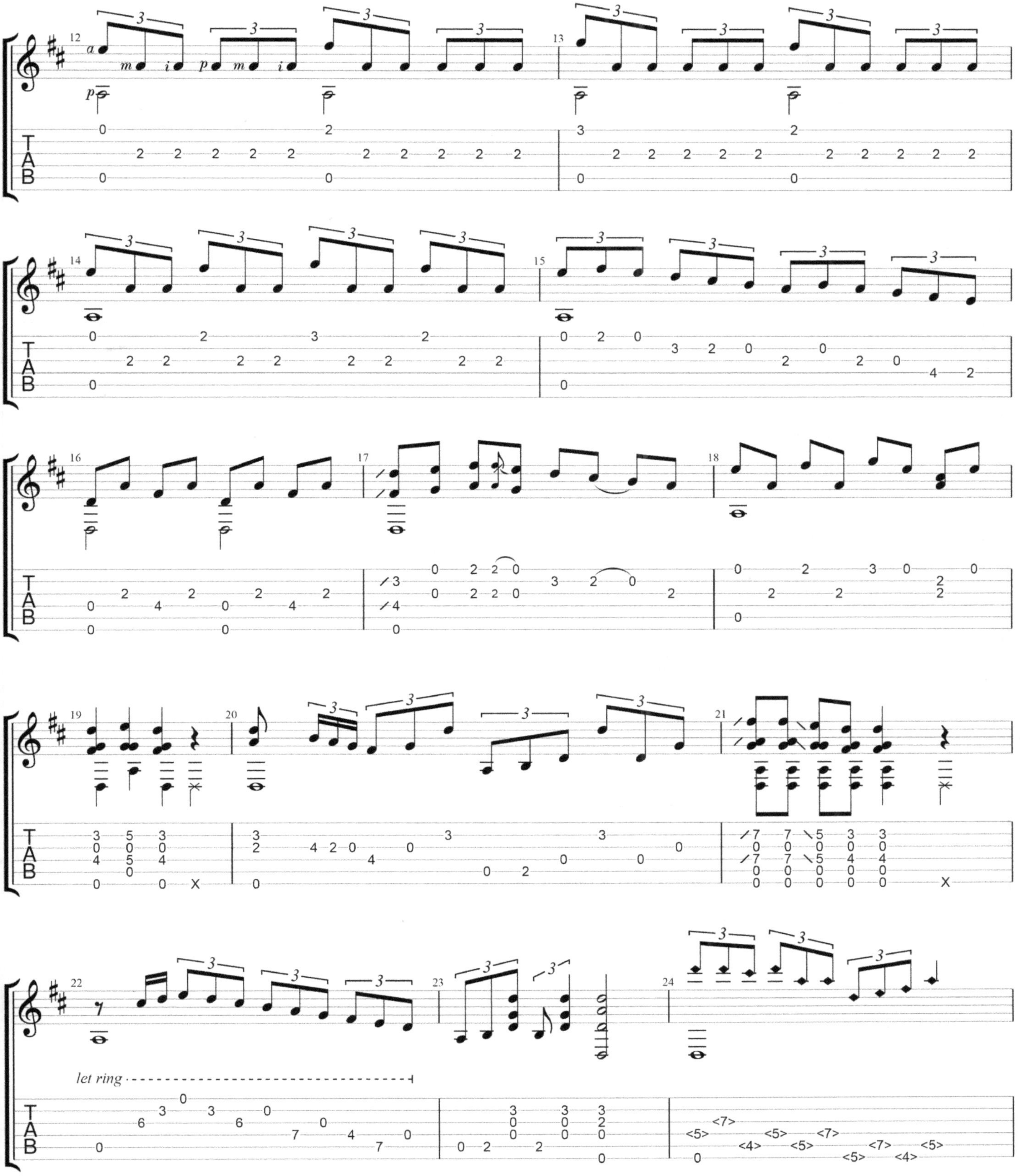
let ring

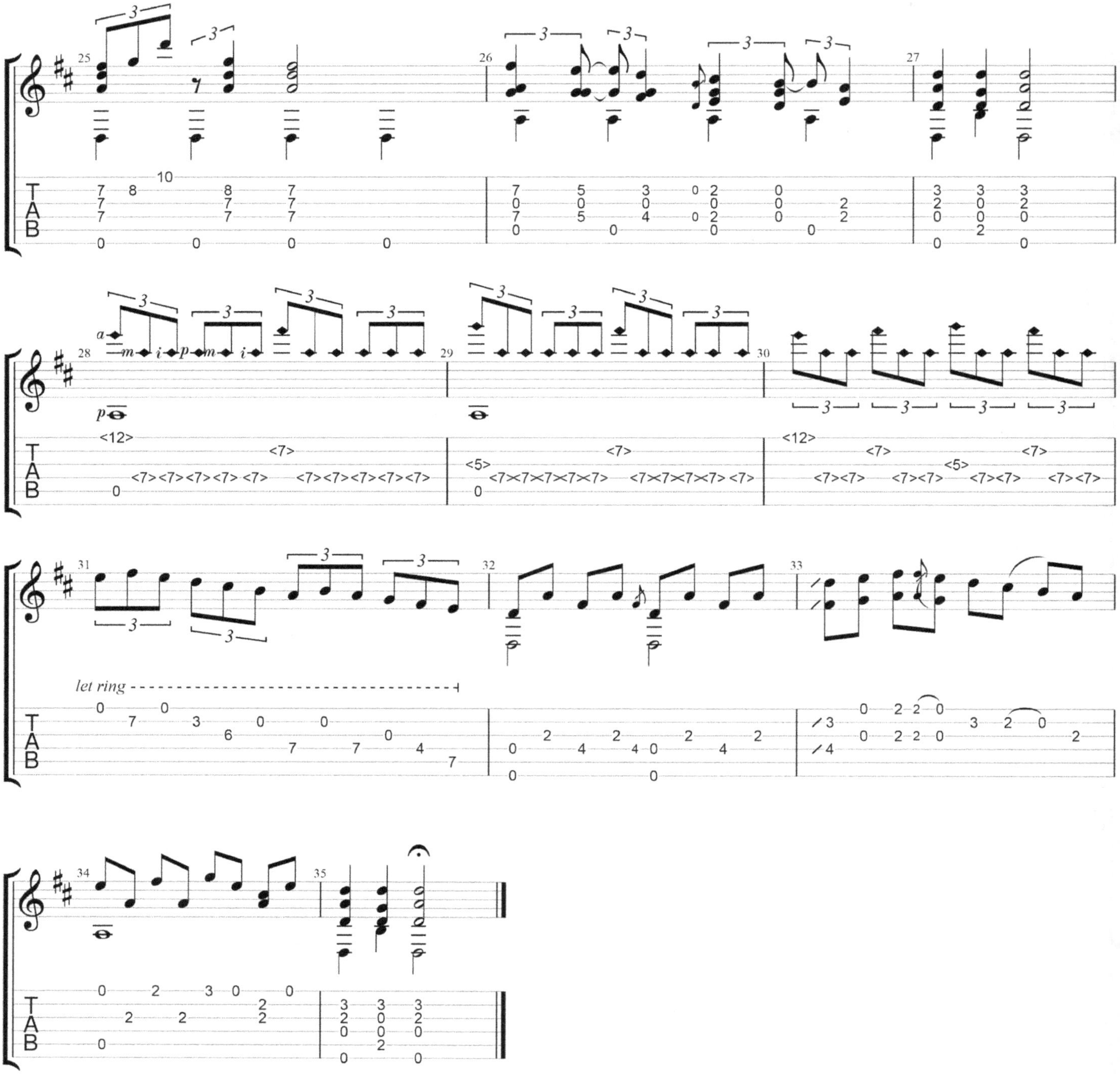
let ring
a m i p m i
p
TAB

Chapter Eleven – I'll Tell Me Ma

I'll Tell Me Ma (also known as *The Belle of Belfast City*) was the accompaniment to a children's game in the 19th Century. The song has since become a popular song in its own right, having been recorded by the likes of The Dubliners and The Corries.

This arrangement is in dropped D tuning. As with the arrangement of *Reilly's Daughter*, the thumb (*p*) plays an alternating pattern on the low strings, with the fingers (*a*, *m* and *i*) playing the melody and chords on the high strings. As with most Travis picking type patterns, I used a thumb pick to record this.

Example 11a

In bar three, the pattern becomes a little more complex. Be sure to stick to the suggested picking hand fingering in the notation.

Example 11b

Hold down the chord shape in bar twelve and pull off the second finger to sound the open string (labelled with "T"). Then keep the remaining notes of the chord held down and sound the harmonic using the picking hand only.

Example 11c

For the chord with a fretted note on the bottom and harmonics on top, fret the note with the first finger and barre the third finger across the 12th fret, lightly touching the node points. Hold this position for the remaining bars in the example.

Example 11d

Now here's the full arrangement…

I'll Tell Me Ma arrangement

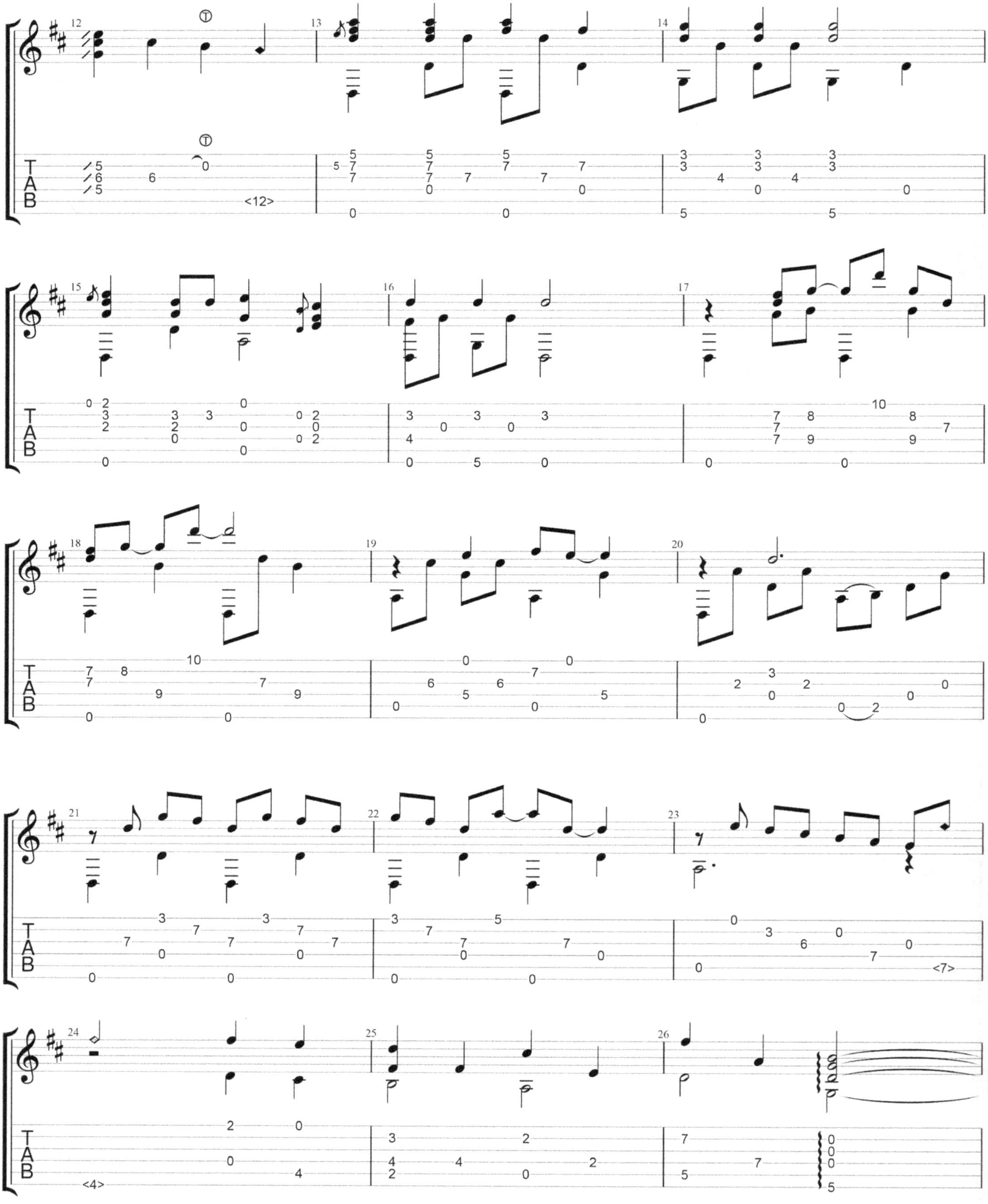

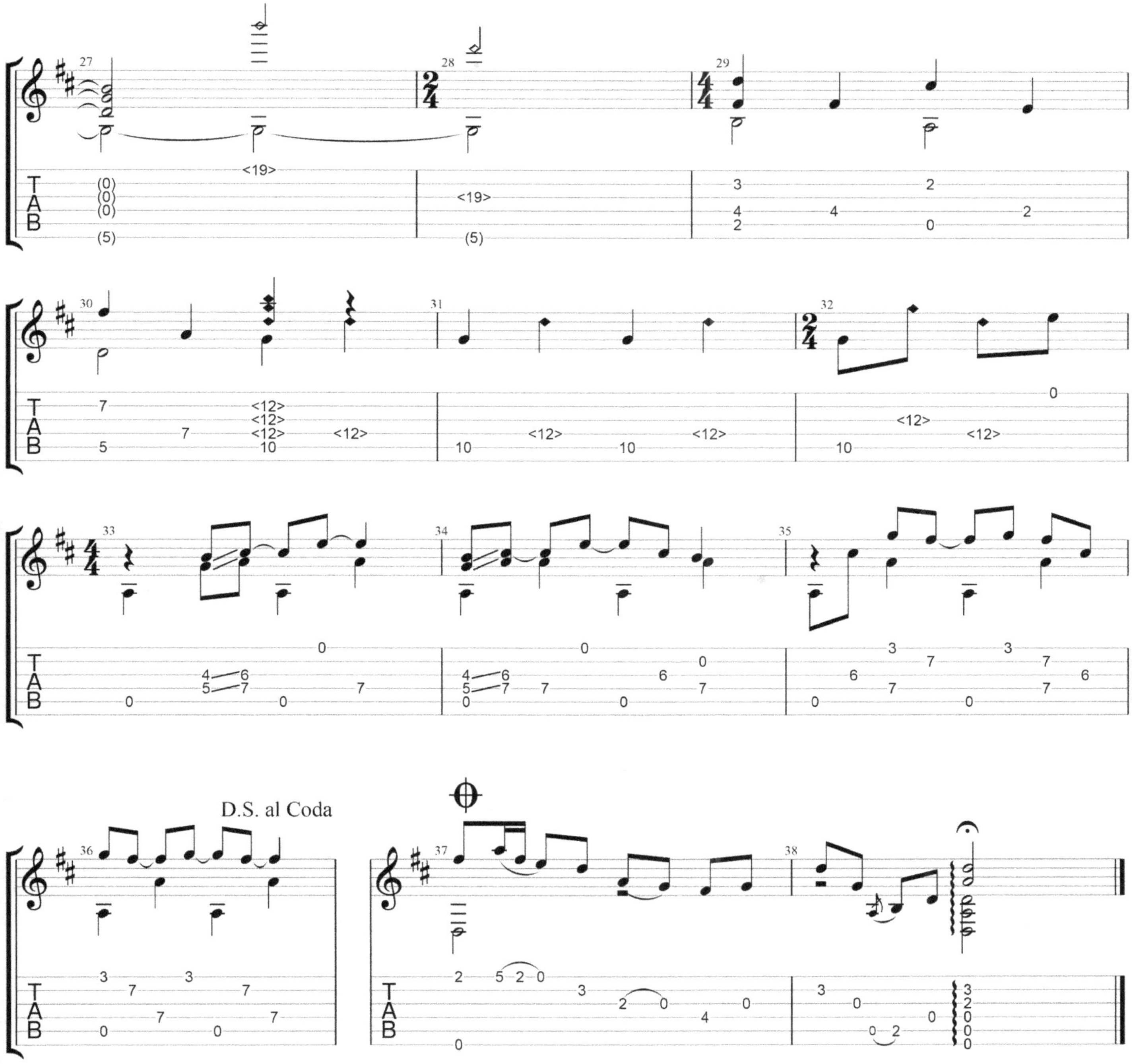
D.S. al Coda
TAB

Chapter Twelve – The Rose of Tralee

The Rose of Tralee is a well-loved 19th Century ballad. The verses tell the story of a man longing to be with his love – a beautiful woman in his homeland called Mary – as he himself is amidst the horrors of war in a strange, foreign land.

This arrangement is in dropped D tuning with a capo at the 4th fret. I used a thumb pick for the recording and have consequently used the thumb more than I would normally, if I was playing without a pick. I haven't included picking hand fingering in the notation, in case you decide not to use one.

In bar thirty-six, fret the fourth string with *m* (middle finger). You can then anchor it here and still have ample fingers for the notes on the first and third strings. Likewise, in bar thirty-eight, use *a* (ring finger) on the sixth string so you can anchor it and have a good position to reach the other notes with the *i* (index) and the pinky finger.

Example 12a

In bar forty-two, the open first string (indicated with a "T") is played by pulling off the *i* (index) finger. After this, pick with a fast *"i, m, a, m, i"* pattern.

Example 12b

Dropped D
⑥ = D

At bar fifty-eight, execute the 7th fret harmonic and the note on the 2nd fret simultaneously by playing the harmonic with just the picking hand while you hammer-on to the 2nd fret with the fretting hand.

Example 12c

Dropped D
⑥ = D

Here is the final full arrangement.

The Rose of Tralee arrangement

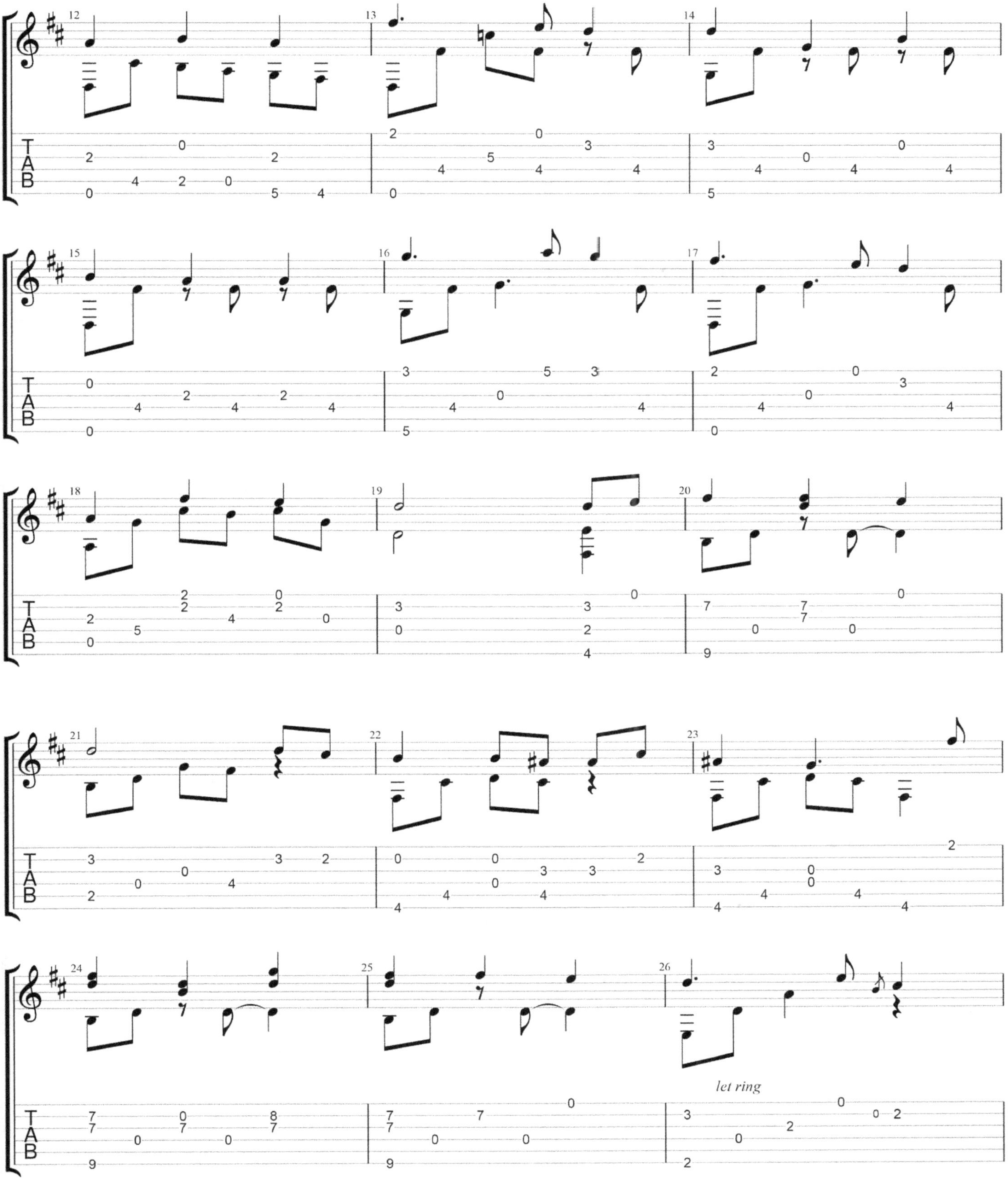
let ring

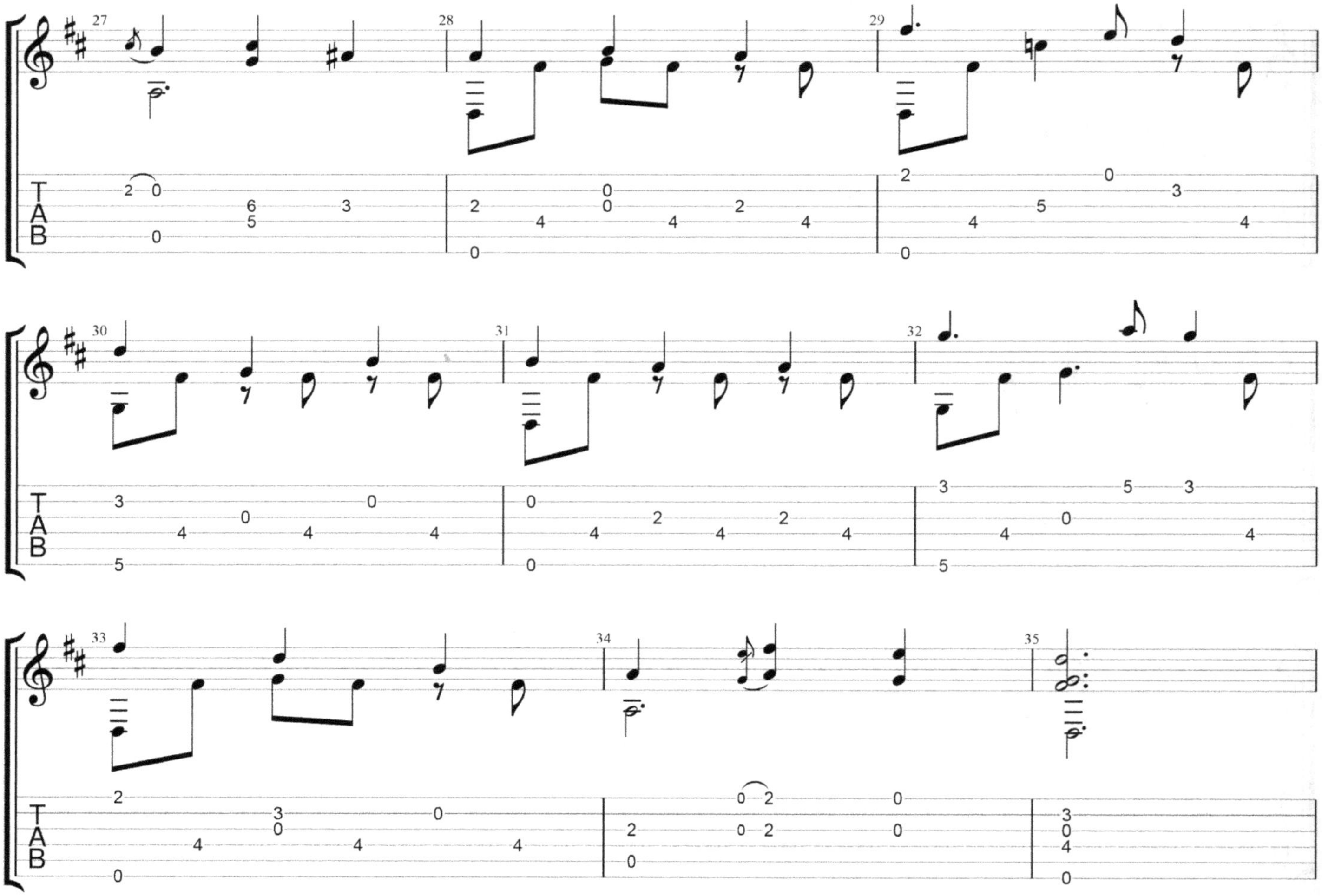

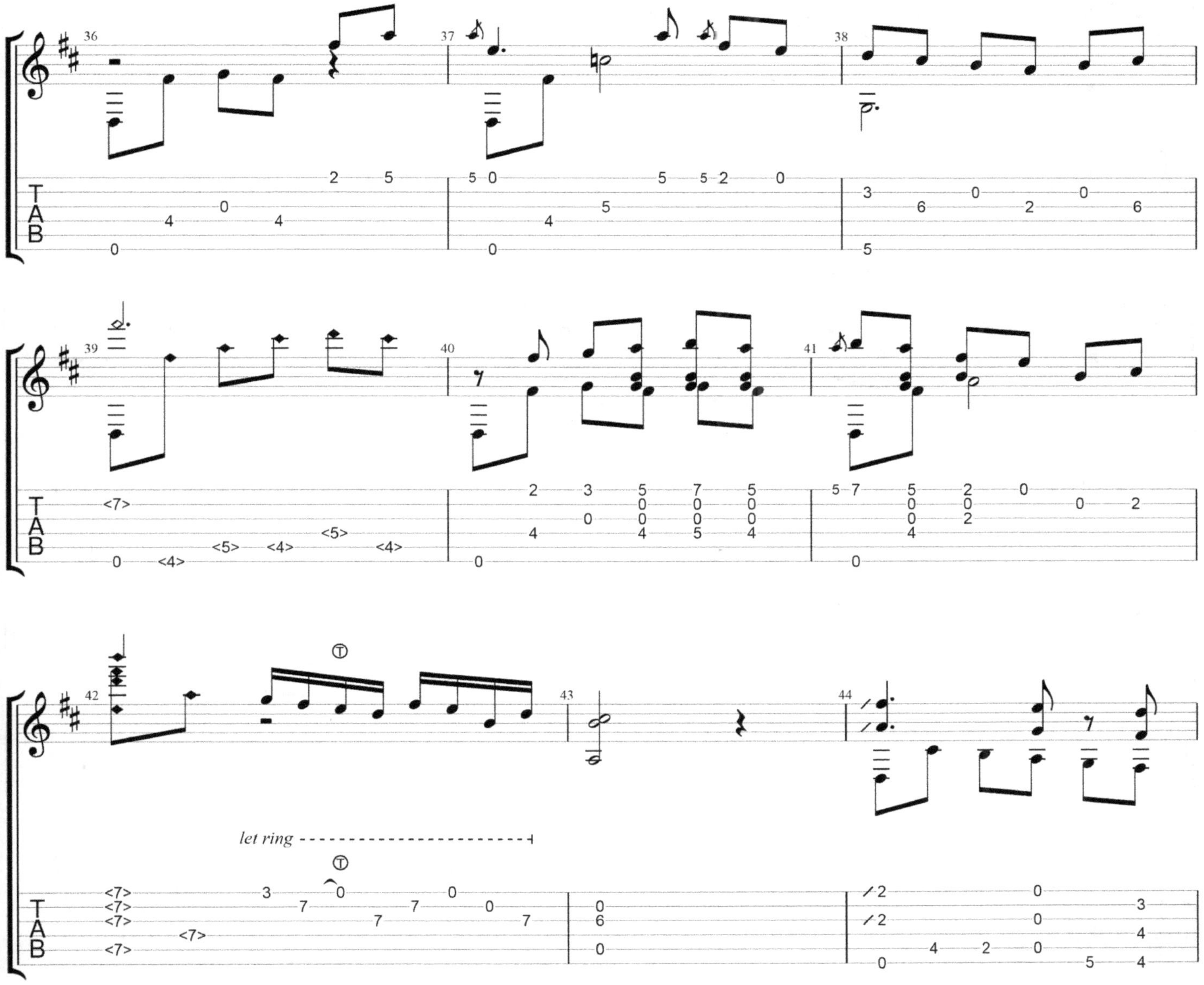
let ring

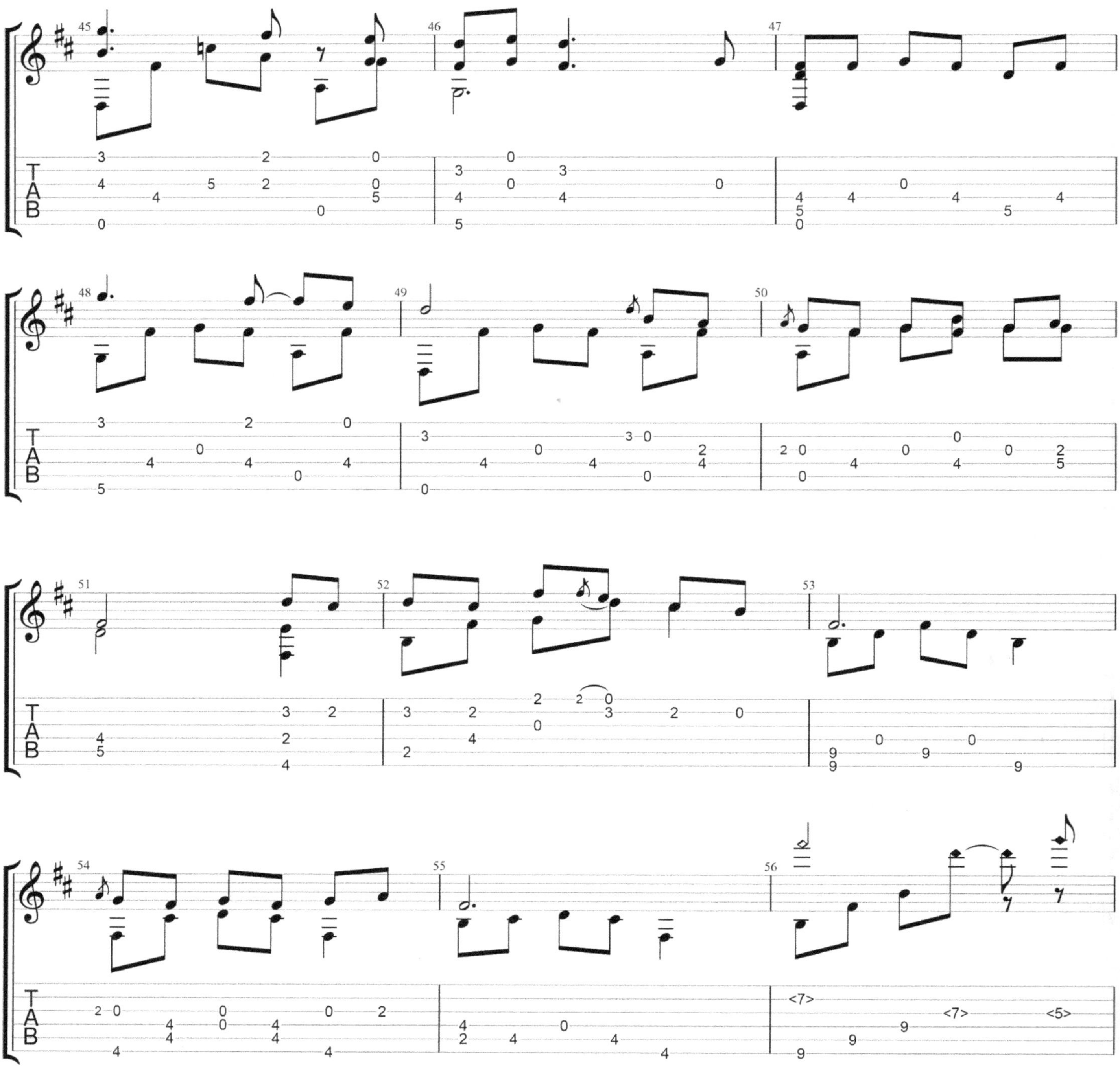

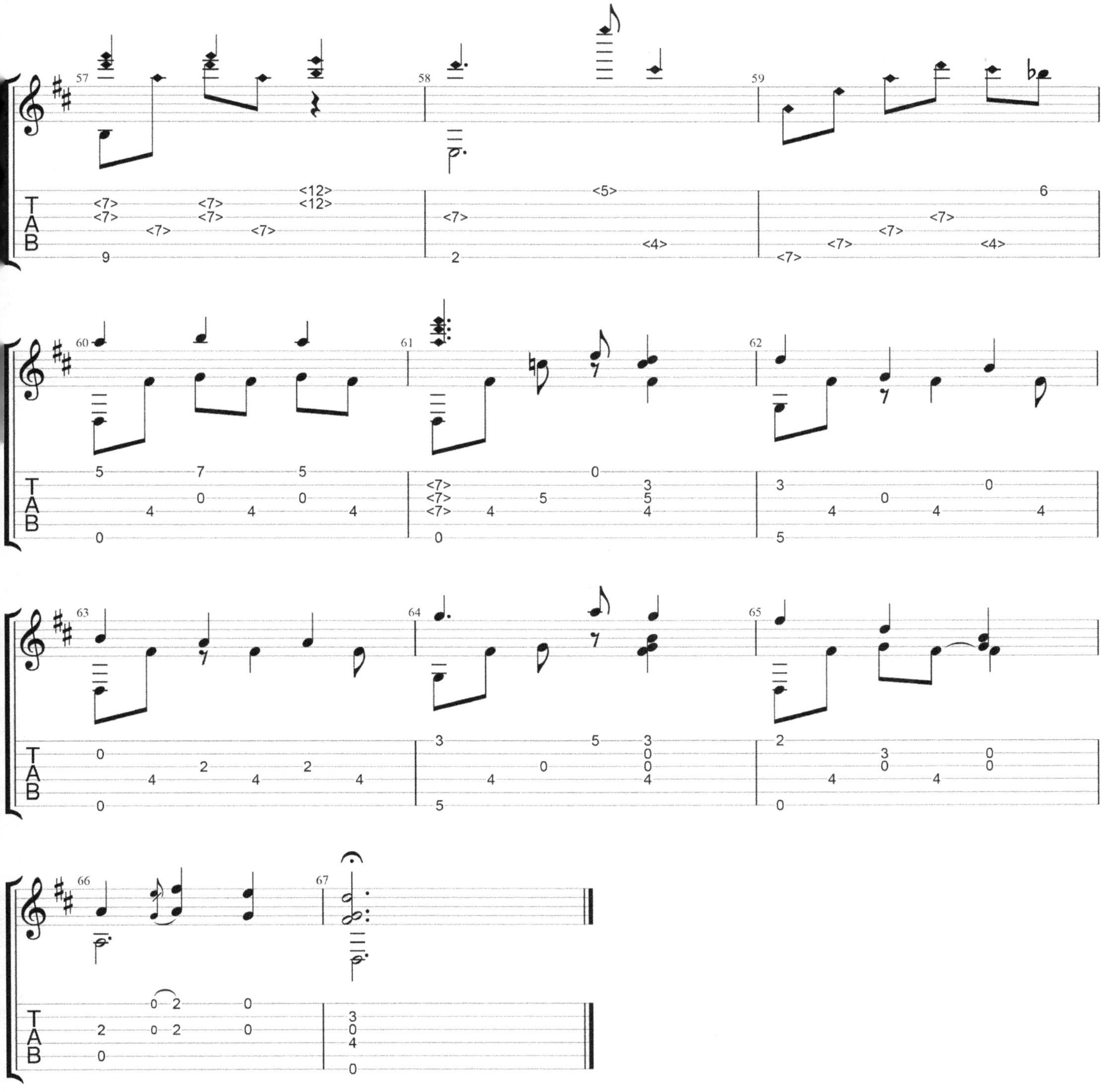